100

LIVESTREAMING & DIGITAL MEDIA PREDICTIONS

VOLUME 2

Top Content Creators Help You Succeed Online in an Era of Rapid Change

ROSS BRAND

livestreamuniverse.com

First published by Livestream Universe
ROSS BRAND
100 LIVESTREAMING & DIGITAL MEDIA PREDICTIONS, Volume 2
Top Content Creators Help You Succeed Online in an Era of Rapid Change

First Edition 2022

DOWNLOAD FULL COLOR EDITION FOR FREE

INCLUDES 130+ IMAGES

As an additional thank you for getting the book, I'd like to give you the full color digital version 100% FREE!

To download, go to the last page in the book.

BONUS

Thank you so much for choosing this book.

I reached out to some of the best brands in the digital space to put together a PDF with special offers and discounts.

Download your copy at:

livestreamuniverse.com/readerbonuses2.

GRATITUDE

ALSO BY ROSS BRAND

100 Livestreaming & Digital Media Predictions (Volume 1), 2021

Winner of Six Book Awards

#1 Amazon Best Seller in 17 Categories

Includes Ross' Interviews with Top Creators

For my parents, Marion & Irv Brand

REACTIONS TO VOLUME 1

"Ross Brand is a visionary and an innovator. An early adopter in the livestreaming space, he's developed a dedicated following because he's an engaging expert on all things livestream—from compelling content to the best value for equipment/gear. Ross has been a game-changer in his commitment to paying his speakers, starting with his first Monetize Livestreaming NOW summit. I was honored to be one of them and a contributor to this book, along with many wonderful personalities in the livestreaming, entertainment, and entrepreneurial space including Winnie Sun, Ja Rule, Steffen Kaplan, Tim Sohn, Valerie Morris, Gord Isman, Kim Doyal, Dale L. Roberts, Elikqitie, and Daniella Malfitano. As Jennifer Quinn "JennyQ" puts it in her inspiring foreward, Ross has "fostered a commitment to collaboration-over-competition among highly individualistic and brand-sensitive speakers." I highly recommend this information-packed, breezy-to-read guide."

-Nancy Ancowitz, author of *Self Promotion for Introverts*®

"If you want to know the future of livestreaming, podcasting, videos, or digital media -- from live shows to live concerts -- you need to dig into this collection. There is a lot of wisdom in this book that should not be overlooked. Trend analysis has always been hit or miss in this industry. Yet, all your market research, industry surveys, or convention conversations cannot hold a microphone to what you will learn in 100 LiveStreaming & Digital Media Predictions by Ross Brand. This book contains the secrets to online success for the next five years. All you need to do is act on it."

-Kyle Bondo, Gagglepod

"This book combines 100 of the top minds in social media, livestreaming and digital media and provides a masterclass on the future of the industry. The author, Ross Brand, is a pillar in the livestreaming world and this book represents the amazing relationships he has formed during his time in livestreaming. This book is packed with insight into the future of all things online content."

-Dan Currier, YouTuber at Creator Fundamentals

"Great collection of wisdom that Ross was able to put together. Glad this community is there to share wisdom."

-Tim Gillette, founder of Simple Easy Events

"Congrats to Ross Brand for putting together a great read and resource for anyone who wonders what the future of livestreaming and digital media is. I mean, if you read this and don't get dozens and dozens of practical ideas, then you're not paying attention...so read it again."

-Kevin Kolbe, YouTuber

"Ross Brand's *100 Livestreaming & Digital Media Predictions* is a must-read for any business owner who wants to drive revenue online. This book is filled with useful tips from the best of the best. It's a gold mine of information you can implement immediately. Kudos to Ross Brand for putting this together."

-Brad Friedman, author of *The Small Business Owner's Guide to Inbound Marketing*

"Ross Brand is known in the online marketing space for being one of the smartest humans around when it comes to not only video/ streaming but when it comes to doing so while making money! He has a knack for finding the best of the best DOERS in their zone of genius and sharing what they've done to get results! If you're truly looking to make a difference in your business using video get this book!"

-Jessika Phillips, president at NOW Marketing Group

"Ross Brand does a fabulous job bringing in expertise from many different fields to hear what is happening today. Livestreaming is hot but it can also be confusing. Ross taps into the genius brain power of many experts who give great ideas that can help us in our own livestreaming. Thank you Ross, for putting this together for us!"

-Terry Brock, Agorapreneurs with Terry Brock

"If you want to be on the cutting edge of Livestreaming, then you must pick up this book. Ross did a great job of interviewing some amazing content creators that have been in the game, some for decades and others just starting out. The interviews are succinct and to the point. This book is easy to consume. Pick up a copy and get one for a friend."

-Meiko Patton, Clubhouse Influencer

"Ross is amazing when it comes to livestreaming, he is always on the cutting edge of the technology and marketing aspect of going live! If you are looking to be at the forefront of this growing digital marketing medium, then you definitely want to grab a copy of Ross's book!"

-Elikqitie, author of *The Guide to Traveling Gluten Free*

"Not only is Ross Brand an incredible pioneer and visionary in the livestreaming space but what he has compiled in this book is a veritable gold mine of experts and online influencers who educate all of us on how we can take our livestreams and digital assets to the next level. If You Want To Grow Your Livestreams This is THE BOOK."

-Professor Nez, author & host of #NezNation

"Ross is one of the most highly-thought-of professionals in the industry. It is clear from the book's content, that the author is one of the most gracious, helpful, humble, well-loved and knowledgeable people that the other contributors are privileged to know. When you read this book, you'll find out why!"

-Stuart Buchan, retired virtual media consultant

"Ross Brand has become one of my go to people for livestreaming information. In this book Ross hits it out of the park. These predictions are a MUST read and would benefit anyone who wants to improve their livestreaming knowledge."

-Robert Cairns, podcaster & digital marketing strategist

"Ross and his contributing experts show you how to create and engage on live video and all the top social media platforms. While anyone can create content, getting that content read, listened to, and watched can be challenging. In this book, you'll learn how to do all this and more from some of the top content creators I know. Get the book, take action, and have fun creating relevant content on trending topics!"

-Mitch Jackson, The Metaverse Lawyer

"100 Livestreaming and Digital-Media Predictions is an insightful read to learn about the world of livestreaming. Ross nicely covers a big picture view of the livestreaming universe as he shares current insights on a variety of topics: monetization of livestreaming, transitioning to virtual events, live summits, livestreaming platforms, vertical video, and livestreaming tech. I found the diversity of predictions to be very inspiring. Doing livestreaming is like next-level video for engaging your audience and building credibility in a highly competitive world. I can't wait to do more livestreaming with guests and bring value to my audience!"

-Gord Isman, YouTuber & Video Consultant

"So many great predictions by so many people of different disciplines. It's fascinating to see everyone's thoughts on the future of livestreaming & digital media after what we've been through over the past couple of years. I look forward to acting on some of these over the next while! Thanks for putting this together, Ross. Really well done!"

-Jodi Krangle, voice actor and audio branding expert

Storytelling in all forms will be more important than ever. The ability to grab a viewer's attention in a short-form video (less than one minute), regular video, or livestream will be critical.

-Andrew Kan

Leaders and hiring professionals will rely heavily on livestreaming and two-way video-based communication tools to reinforce company culture, keep current employees fully informed, and candidates inspired.

-Mark S. Babbitt

TABLE OF CONTENTS

FOREWORD BY DALE L. ROBERTS

In 1994, three college students invented a game known as *Six Degrees of Kevin Bacon*. Impressed by the famous actor's prolific film work, the students developed this game based on Kevin Bacon as the center of the entertainment universe. The theory surrounds the actor working with so many people in show business that he's had contact with everyone imaginable. Every celebrity has up to six degrees of separation from Kevin Bacon. Even you and I could navigate through our virtual Rolodex to find some contact who worked with someone who knows Kevin Bacon.

That's why we can all agree, Ross Brand is the Kevin Bacon of livestreaming and digital media marketing. Ross isn't the type to toot his own horn, so I'll do it for him. Deeply entrenched in broadcast media for most of his life - whether radio or online video – Ross solidified his legacy in the annals of livestreaming history. Anyone who has the pleasure of meeting Ross can understand why. He's a warm, compassionate, and genuine dude. Now, I have to stop all the compliments, otherwise this foreword will seem forced, and Ross' head will grow larger than it should be. I assure you, I'm writing this of my own freewill.

Ross has hosted hundreds of live broadcasts with thousands of guests. Whether working with a small business owner or chatting it up with famous influencers, he has a front row view of every angle in entrepreneurship. His diverse panels of guests and ability to interview like a top-tier professional are unparalleled. Seriously, after appearing multiple times in his long-running video series, Livestream Universe, I have shared the screen with some pretty big superstars.

Let me dial it back a bit and tell you why this isn't just a flex. Nope, I'm merely sharing facts. Over the past seven years, Ross curated the most well-known and best-kept secrets in the land of livestreaming video and digital media. He leverages his network of friends and showcases their keen insights on the business.

Each guest expert comes with boat loads of experience and insights that only come from being a mainstay in their respective field. Why should their opinions matter? The contributors in this book all live, breathe, and consume digital media. With years of practice and time in this arena, they can identify patterns. If 1+1=2, and 2+2=4, then 4+4=8. Right? I wish it were as simple and accurate as remedial math problems. That's why I lay trust in what they say, then do my research on how much weight their advice carries.

Contained in this book, you'll find one hundred contributions serving as a snapshot frozen in a time capsule. As the years go on, we can go back and review the predictions. That's when things get exciting. Similar to opening the old high school yearbook, you get to reminisce about fun times. Why was my hair permed? Was my lazy eye getting a divorce with my good eye? And did I really take part in all those clubs? We can all have a few laughs, but there's a much stronger reason to read this book.

The most powerful thing to come of it is when we say,

"Hey, remember when (insert subject) was a thing?"

or

"Remember when they first announced the news about the (insert topic)?"

Why do you need the latest *100 Livestreaming & Digital Media Predictions*? How will these predictions impact your life?

Consider weather forecasts. Are they ever 100% accurate? Possibly not, but at least you leave the house making an informed decision. You can go outside with an umbrella as a safeguard. Should you run into rainfall, you're prepared to take cover. Then again, what if you don't take the umbrella? As you'd expect, you're taking the chance of getting soaked by the rain. I don't know about you, but I like to stay dry unless I'm taking a shower.

Rather than leave your future with a giant question mark over it, why not consider the possibilities? Fortunately for you, the answers are in your hands. All you have to do is turn the page and dig right in.

Ross Brand may not be King of the Silver Screen, but he sure fits the equivalent role in the livestreaming community. Many livestreamers and digital media marketers respect him. This book is proof. Look at all the contributors!

Sadly, Ross only has three degrees of separation from Kevin Bacon. I'm sure he'd love to skip straight to one degree, but he's going to have to call in a few favors to make that happen. In case you were wondering…

Ross Brand interviewed Ja Rule who starred in "Scary Movie 3" with Denise Richards who starred in "Wild Things" with Kevin Bacon.

The good news is you only have one degree of separation between Ross and his one-hundred contributors. It's in your hands and gracing your eyeballs. Pull up a seat, kick back, and open the book wherever your heart desires. You can read this cover-to-cover or simply in small snippets. The choice is yours. In the meantime, be safe and have fun!

-Dale L. Roberts
Livestreaming Advocate, Award-Winning Author

PART I
THE BIG PICTURE

INTRODUCTION

When it comes to digital media, the best way to build an audience, grow your business and strengthen your brand is through the quality of your content. That was true when I started livestreaming in 2015 and it remains true today, even as the landscape and tools drastically change.

In livestreaming, it's the host that draws us in and keeps us engaged. With online courses, it's the educator that demands our attention. For digital audio, it's the podcaster that makes us want to listen again and again. On a blog, the talent of the writer and the utility of his or her tips keeps our eyes on the page.

It all starts with you, the creator. See an increase in results from digital media by refining your talent and developing the professional skills to deliver informative and entertaining content. When you uplevel your approach to creating, you set yourself apart from the thousands of interview streams, personal interest podcasts and educational blogs. You have what it takes to turn your high-quality content into an engaged and loyal community.

Strategically monetize by offering products and services (your own and affiliate) aligned with the needs of your audience. When presented with tact or humor, consumers of your audio, video and written output accept your efforts at generating revenue. The platforms are making money from your content, why not you?

But talent and quality can't win without strategy. Even your most amazing talents and greatest pieces of content won't just magically find audiences and advance your business objectives. You need the strategies to put YOU in front of people in this fast-changing digital landscape.

That's why every year since 2016, we gather leading creators and entrepreneurs to share their forecasts, insights and strategies to grow and engage audiences and employ new technology. Learn to invest your time in those mediums and platforms that are positively impacting businesses.

It's more difficult than it used to be to get traction online for your digital content. Platforms like Facebook Live and LinkedIn Live, that at one time seemed to notify a large percentage of your network when you hit the go live button, now only alert a small portion of your friends and followers. In the early to mid 2010s, Twitter was the place to connect and grow your network through text conversations. Now, outside of real-time Tweeting on breaking news and live events, many users are automating their accounts. Your promotional and informational posts on most major social platforms aren't getting the same reach either.

The book's contributors share a wide range of digital media, technical and business strategies to advance the overall impact and reach of your content. They help you overcome the challenges discussed above with insights to pinpoint the best opportunities for you to thrive. I highly recommend paying attention to the tools and tactics discussed in the 100 predictions, 30 additional strategy entries and the extensive resources section in the back of the book.

There are new and amazing opportunities for livestreamers. Before turning over the pages to our all-star panel of digital creators and online entrepreneurs who cover a wide range of content mediums, here is my advice to anyone who wants to succeed with livestreaming in the current environment:

1. Work on your hosting skills. Nothing -- and I mean nothing -- goes further to bring in viewers, build relationships and impact your business than your hosting skills. Your ability to inform, educate, entertain, engage, advance the conversation and deliver with credibility are all among the things that will help you cut through the digital noise.

2. Leverage the "portfolio method" to close warm leads. Think of livestreaming as a way to quickly create a large volume of content. Put less importance on how many people watch, comment or share. Focus on creating high-quality content that you can later repurpose on your website, YouTube channel, Facebook page and Instagram account. Put the repurposed content anywhere that audiences are likely to go to learn about you. It doesn't have to mean using the whole recording, but even a short clip helps you to close warm leads, land clients and get jobs.

3. Look at alternative ways to monetize that don't depend on the volume of viewers on a public platform. Consider putting your livestreams behind a paywall targeted to a small group of people who are seeking exclusive content such as courses or memberships. Look at livestreaming as a way to provide access for people to ask you questions, get help in real-time and engage with you through live videos in a private environment.

4. Livestream on shopping platforms like Amazon Live. Develop your skillset for selling on live video. You will see more shopping platforms

add livestreaming for selling products and services, including through in-stream purchasing features. You can also repurpose portions of those videos talking about a product to help drive sales on Amazon product pages or upload them to YouTube with a link in the description.

That's my two cents. Now, let's get to the predictions!

Thank you to our all-star panelists for providing their thoughtful answers.

Happy Streaming!

PART II
PREDICTIONS

1. Winnie Sun

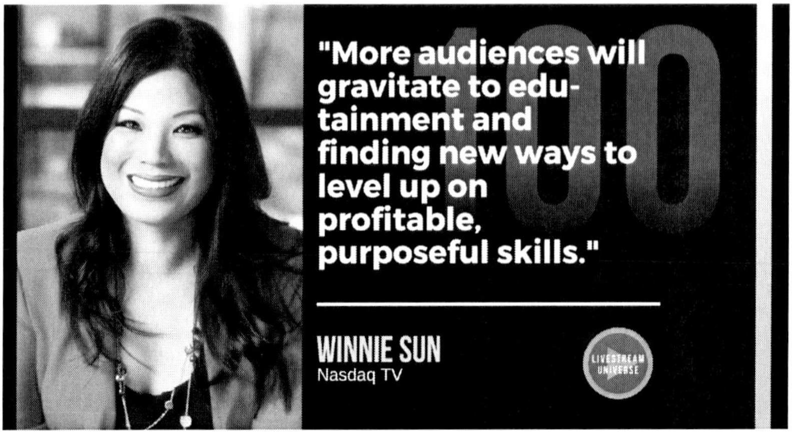

2022 is going to be the year of working smarter, not harder. More audiences will gravitate to edu-tainment and finding new ways to level up on profitable, purposeful skills. The power of livestreaming will just get greater. Timely, on-demand content, by trusted voices is key.

The key term today is convenience. Traditional newspapers, classrooms are replaced by video, audio, and more. For brands and leadership it will mean that their content will evolve to classifications, i.e. – leisure vs. status/degree/specialization content. The definition of quality will continue to evolve. And, style and content will have to differentiate to remain sustainable.

Media and social media platforms will continue to contract, and success in this space is only going to get more expensive to compete. And, in turn, the loyal, engaged audience just becomes even more valuable.

#WinnieSun has been shared over 25B times (March 2021). Winnie is one of the most influential, award-winning voices in the financial industry. Forbes contributor, CNBC council member, and more.

2. JEFFREY FITZGERALD

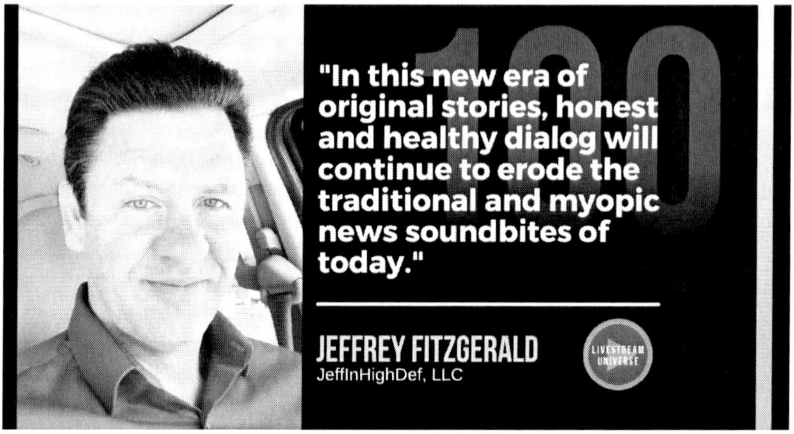

No doubt our world is on fire, and one thing is certain: everyone is talking – but absolutely no one is listening. To make matters worse, the continued villainization of opposing viewpoints has rendered government and society ill-equipped to ever move forward again. Something that's evidenced by every election cycle. That no matter the winner, we all lose when we choose to pick a party instead of a wealth of perspectives.

So, what could possibly be a viable prediction in this predicament? I believe livestreaming holds the answer for all of us. In 2022, content creators will embrace more issue-driven content with authentic community conversations.

Venturing beyond the familiar pillars of mindset and marketing, some will move into shows that seek greater understanding from a wider variety of voices. All through true discourse and dialog. And yes, the civil kind between people who neither look or think like you. Gathered in tiny square video boxes together, sharing experiences that may no longer contain all the past perceptions and agendas. Just great conversation.

Livestreaming has already embodied itself as a bastion of next-generation citizen journalism. From revealing the tragedy of George Floyd to showing us the kindness of strangers. What many today see mainly as a marketing tool, just might change our world… or our neighborhood. And both are valuable.

I believe these content creators not only embrace the questions of our day, but do so with genuine interest over predictable single-sided activism. Which offers all of us the ability to listen, learn and hopefully interact with those experiences we know very little.

In the end, I think one day the influx of new perspectives – and maybe even newly found future leaders from all walks of life – will usher in a broader sense of greater meaning and purpose. And with it, in this new era of original stories, honest and healthy dialog will continue to erode the traditional and myopic news soundbites of today.

Jeffrey Fitzgerald of JeffinHighDef is a 25-year veteran of streaming and online video, entering his 40th year in broadcast. He currently provides broadcast and digital marketing for America's volunteer first responders and is a 2020 two-time Emmy Award Winning Producer.

3. Madeleine Smithberg

The way things are going with covid, it may be a while until we need to put pants on. Meanwhile, my kitchen has been transformed into a virtual production studio. I guess I will not get out of my house in 2022, but I will keep creating entertaining and delicious content. (And I do wear pants.)

At the age of 60, Madeleine Smithberg pivoted from her career as an executive producer of comedy television (Emmy and Peabody Award-winning co-creator of THE DAILY SHOW) and followed her life-long passion for cooking and began working as a chef. She launched the MAD IN THE KITCHEN YouTube channel during Covid on an iPhone – now she has 4 cameras, a switcher, and professional lighting and audio. She's been on the TODAY SHOW 3 times, and has a deal to develop a show.

4. Dale L. Roberts

More video creators and online entrepreneurs have additional options in monetizing their brands, especially in livestreaming. Sure, between NFTs, NFT Gaming, and Crypto Gaming, anyone can get a bigger slice of the pie. However, I couldn't tell you how that works and where someone would start.

What I do see happening is the explosion of self-publishing in the video creator community. More influencers than ever are self-publishing books to provide an additional stream of revenue while passively marketing through various online retailers including the massive online juggernaut, Amazon. Now that newer influencers are coming out, they're acutely aware of their options and what a self-published book can do for revenue and free marketing. Why now? Because you don't have to throw a rock before you hit an article, video, blog or social media post showcasing self-published books or teaching how simple the process can be.

Sure, this seems rather suspect coming from the guy who's been the go-to in the self-publishing community. However, I've been in the video creator space since 2016. The longer I'm in the space, the more creators I see launching new publications that represent their brand while generating passive revenue. How do we quantify this amount? How will we know how many creators self-publish a book year over year? Simple, we don't. Just look around within the video creator and influencer space. Then, monitor it for a year and you'll find out whether or not I'm right. Or, if you are one of the people who has NOT published a book, then skip collecting data and publish a book instead.

Dale L. Roberts is an award-winning and bestselling author who's deeply passionate about writing and publishing books. He's also the host of three fully-monetized YouTube Channels in Self-Publishing with Dale, The Self-Publishing with Dale Podcast, and Livestreaming Tech.

5. Kirk Nugent

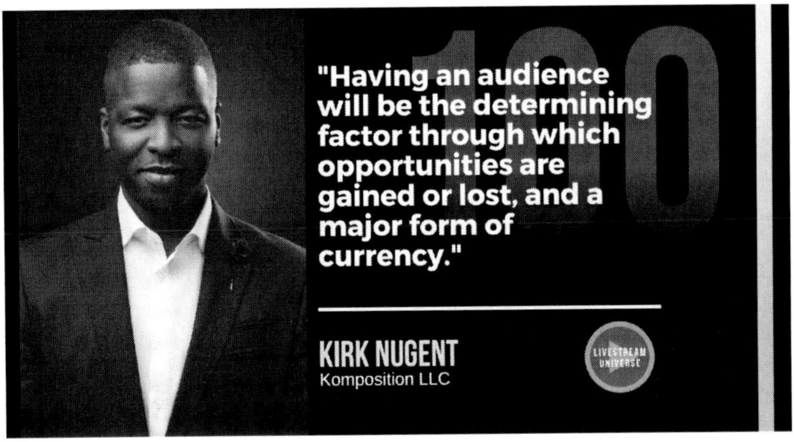

One of the consistent motivators for aspiring and even established Content Creators is the ability to support ourselves financially. For some the focus is growing a following, for others the drive is to establish themselves as a thought leader, but for the vast majority, even those who fall into either of those categories, the core motivation is financial freedom. How can we support ourselves with the knowledge we have? So we create videos, memes, blog posts, podcasts, live streams, courses, conferences, to be able to monetize our knowledge but there is a fringe benefit some, but not all, have ignored.

A benefit that I predict will become a major form of currency rivaling industries and even blockchain: Audience. Audience growth, in our circles, is mentioned more as a representation of earning potential but I predict that we will see a shift in 2022 where having an Audience will be the determining factor through which opportunities are gained or lost. Audience will become a major, if not the top, form of Currency.

Kirk Nugent of Koposition LLC teaches Businesses and Leaders how to gain Visibility and Authority through Live Video Marketing. He's a Remote Producer, Live Video Coach, Content Creation Facilitator, Online Church Consultant and Tech/Media Speaker.

6. Kim Doyal

Newsletters are going to continue to grow, with more and more options to monetize, whether it's through paid subscriptions (we'll see more options from email service providers for this – much like ConvertCommerce), sponsorships, tip jars, and classifieds. I don't think we're too far off from Web 3.0 options for newsletters as well (think NFTs with newsletters). Very exciting times!

Kim Doyal teaches you how to #FtheHUSTLE. Build and scale an online business in a way that works for YOU. Email marketing and newsletters are her sweet spot.

7. Jon Burk

Television is at a tipping point. With the next-gen of content consumption dictated firmly around digital and streaming VOD by "cord nevers," the explosion of AVOD's and FASTs will replace traditional and broadcast TV as we know it. The coming year will see more channels popping up to serve this audience and grab their share of the programmatic advertising pie (AVOD/FAST content is ad-driven with content creators/IP owners splitting revenue with the streaming platform). Thus, discovery and search will be the most important components of this new digital transformation (just like it was with the early days of YouTube and currently, with TikTok).

The streaming platforms that are best able to aggregate and organize content while reducing any friction for viewers to access it, will win viewer loyalty. But that's not enough. Original content is the not-so-secret sauce that allows all platforms – both SVOD and AVOD – to thrive and attract new audiences. Some AVOD's are already populating their channels with original ad-supported content and expect this to explode in the coming year. FAST platforms (like The Roku Channel) will also step up and invest in original programming, making the need for discovery and search imperative.

Jon Burk is the director of digital strategy & marketing for award-winning Al Roker Entertainment, managing the production and activation of digital content and social video for TV programs and branded entertainment produced by the company.

8. Louise McDonnell

The use of short-form Reel style videos exploded in 2021. This style of short engaging fast-moving video is effective at catching and holding the viewers' attention. Use TikTok and Instagram Reels to ramp up your video production skills!! Then apply these techniques to your main streams and video ads. My prediction for 2022 is the brands that adopt this strategy will run more successful, higher-converting social media campaigns.

Louise McDonnell is a Social Media Author, Speaker and Strategist. She's the founder of Sell On Social Media Academy.

9. Nick Nimmin

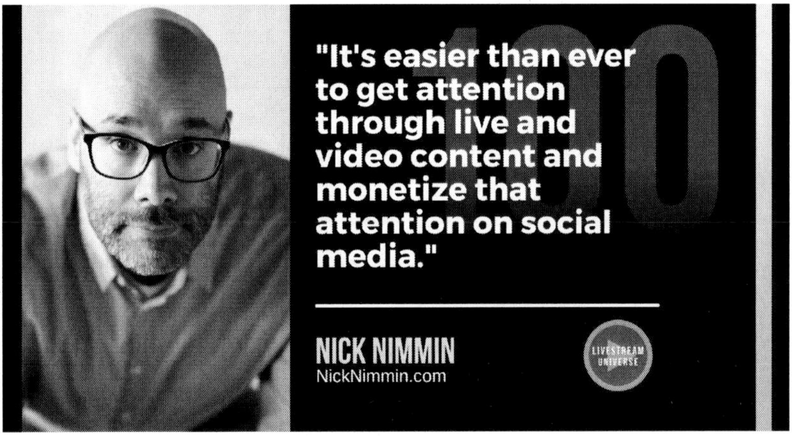

Livestreaming and content creation in general are going to continue to increase as they have been for years I believe we're still in the very early stages of this. With tools like Streamyard completely removing the learning curve it's now easier than ever to jump into streaming. In addition to the barrier to entry evaporating, it's easier than ever to get attention through live and video content and monetize that attention on social media, which also makes it more sustainable to be a content creator, regardless of genre, than it has ever been.

My prediction for 2022 is that we'll have even more tools and resources coming online to serve this ever-growing community of creators which will continue to make things even easier and more efficient. Because of that, we'll see more "new" people leveraging video and streaming content to make an impact in the world and connect with others.

Nick Nimmin teaches content creators how to thrive on YouTube at nicknimmin.com.

10. Jodi Krangle

Audio is IT. We're starting to use our voices for more and more things including the operation of our smart homes, our phones, and our social media (Clubhouse, Greenroom, Twitter Spaces, etc.). That trend will only continue and grow stronger. There is power in the human voice – and it forms far stronger connections between us than the written word. I've gotten to know people much more fully on Clubhouse even after following them for many years on other social media that's visual only.

We're at a crucial point in our technology development where things are simplifying rather than getting more complicated – and what's more simple than our own voices? This will bring some issues we'll have to take care of, however. For instance, Deep Fakes and unauthorized use of our voices, bad actors who will use such things to their advantage. Just because something CAN be done, doesn't mean it SHOULD be. But it will also come with more protections and standards as we realize the toothpaste is already out of the tube. We'll need to build in silent watermarks and ways to track usage – and we will, I have no doubt.

When it comes to audio for businesses, they'll need to harness the power of sound so that they can differentiate themselves from their competitors in audio-only environments. Having a recognizable audio brand – knowing your brand "voice" – and using it consistently across many touchpoints will be key. Start an audio brand NOW so that your advertising doesn't need to work so hard at making you memorable!

Jodi Krangle has been a voice actor since 2007 and has worked with clients from major brands all over the world including Dell, BBVA and Kraft. She's also a singer with her own album of jazz, blues and traditional tunes (jodikranglemusic.com} and has studied sound and how it influences people (her podcast on the subject is called Audio Branding: The hidden gem of marketing).

11. PJ Taei

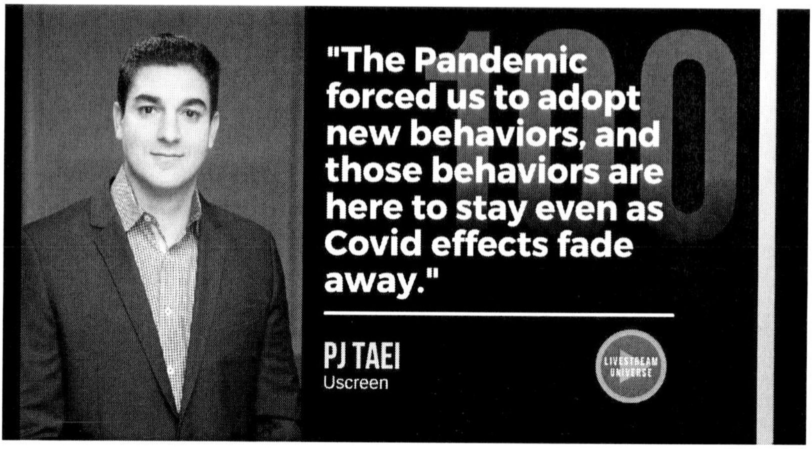

Livestreaming will continue to expand with increased engagement. The pandemic forced us to adopt new behaviors, and those behaviors are here to stay even as covid effects fade away.

PJ Taei is the founder of Uscreen, a video monetization platform helping over 10,000 creators to sell videos online.

12. JENNIFER QUINN (JENNYQ)

With most social platforms heavily favoring generating revenue for the platform (i.e., selling on livestream, tagging products in posts, running ads, etc....) it's even more important than ever for business owners and entrepreneurs to get clear on what their goal is for digital marketing. Since 2008 people have been trying to be everywhere and that simply is not going to work in 2022. It's time to get VERY CLEAR on what your goals are, otherwise, you will get swallowed by those who know. Choose your digital lane and perfect it.

All digital marketing is about creating. In this creator economy, decide how you are going to show up and what you're going to create. And master it. 1. Identify your niche 2. Research where your ideal client is hanging out 3. Go ALL IN on creating content for that platform.

You cannot be all things to all people, and that's okay – it's time to dial in who you want to show up for. And when you do – create the content that makes your ideal client feel seen, heard, and validated. THAT will make you win the 2022 digital marketing game.

Jennifer Quinn, known by her followers as JennyQ, is a podcaster, digital marketing expert, live-streaming pro and champion of her life story. She helps companies "Be Seen" with compelling video-driven content. Now, she's using those talents to help individuals "Be Seen" with resources to transform their life. Join the journey to learn how "Being Seen" can empower your evolution.

13. Mark S. Babbitt

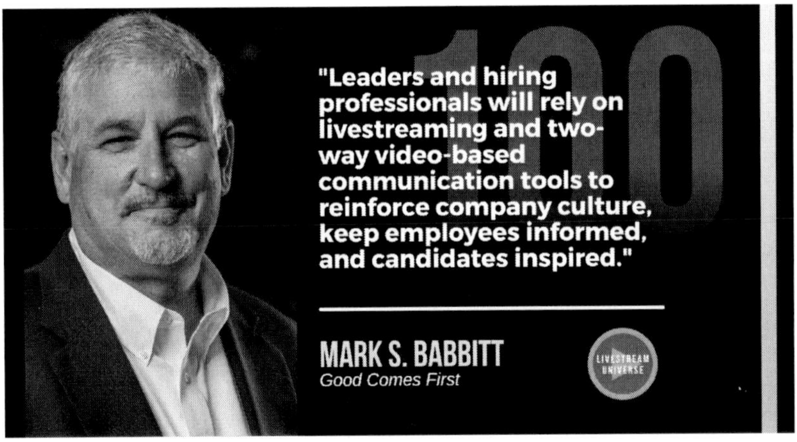

Communication = Culture. While doing research for our book, Good Comes First, one issue came up frequently: Frustration caused by a distinct lack of top-down communication. Unfortunately, in too many companies, this has always been the case.

However, during the pandemic — when employees needed to hear from company leaders most — people working from home felt a lack of direction. Worse yet, many suffered from a deep sense of isolation. Even as employers execute their return-to-work strategies, the best leaders won't take this lesson for granted. Nor will the HR teams tasked with filling the holes left by those employees who left during The Great Reckoning.

Instead, these leaders and hiring professionals will rely heavily on livestreaming and two-way video-based communication tools to reinforce company culture, keep current employees fully informed, and candidates inspired. Digitally — what we now routinely accept as "face-to-face" — they'll build a positive, productive culture by showing the respect employees have earned, validating the contributions of all stakeholders, and steering applicants toward what is possible. And those leaders who don't? When the post-pandemic recovery finally realizes its full potential, those companies will fall even further behind.

Mark S. Babbitt is a speaker, author, blogger, culture architect, executive coach, career mentor, and co-author of "Good Comes First: How Today's Leaders Create an Uncompromising Culture That Doesn't Suck." He serves as President of WorqIQ and CEO and Founder of YouTern.

14. ILEANE SMITH

In 2022, new tools will be developed to serve creators and the booming creator economy. I think we'll see a plethora of apps that we can use for automating our workflows through innovations in AI & AR. It will be a challenge to decide which ones are best at helping us reach our goals. We can look forward to innovations that can revolutionize the way we complete projects from start-to-finish. Exciting times ahead are in store for us all.

Ileane Smith's goal is to provide top-level livestreaming, podcasting, and digital media tutorials to inspire you on your content creation journey.

15. Mitch Jackson

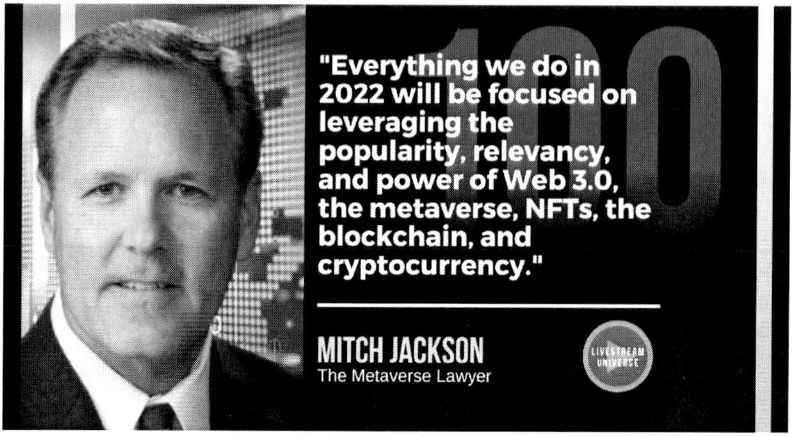

Web 3.0, the Metaverse, NFT, Blockchain, and Cryptocurrency: Everything my firm is doing moving forward in 2022 is focused on leveraging the popularity, relevancy, and power of the metaverse, Web 3.0, NFTs, the blockchain, and cryptocurrency. To help define our brand and exceed our client expectations, we've been wrapping our arms around this evolving technology and will continue to do so for years to come.

My team and I are so passionate about this significant shift in how we live, do business and communicate, that we've rolled out a new legal department in the metaverse. Creators and business owners can now meet with us using virtual reality so that we can easily and quickly help them navigate the fast-changing legal issues. We're using Spatial.io and Horizon Workrooms to create these micro-metaverse VR experiences.

At the same time, every personalized video or social audio project, content, or show that we create and produce will incorporate one or more components of this new digital reality. Books, blog posts, podcasts, social audio, and videos will be shared in our virtual spaces (private offices, conference rooms, and public presentation halls). During and after sessions, consumers can click on any digital assets to immediately be taken or transported to the additional content or desired experience presented in VR.

NFT's are available to all clients. Private and unlockable content and access to firm resources will be customized and made available. QR codes (QR Code Generator) will make sharing and connecting more effortless than ever. While every VR experience is maximized with an Oculus Quest 2 headset, to be as inclusive as possible, we're integrating VR platforms that allow clients to use their phone, tablet, laptop, or desktop to engage and participate.

Most of our products and services already include cryptocurrency options, including payments with Strike (think of Venmo for Bitcoin) and digital wallets like MetaMask. Instead of a client being forced to type our long 42 character public MetaMask wallet address, we use a domain service to make it easier for the consumer to transfer funds. Now all they need to do is send funds to mitchjackson.eth (we used ENS.domains). Keeping things simple results in more engagement and a better client experience.

We'll complement the above with more social audio on Clubhouse and Twitter Spaces. Recorded and live video will also continue to play a big part in our marketing and branding. To respect today's consumers' limited time and attention (everyone is super busy– we get that), our content will be short and created around a specific and relevant compelling story. Across all of our platforms, including what happens in the metaverse, we plan on using many of Casey Neistat's storytelling techniques.

To create better video experiences, we're using Bombbomb to personalize email video messages and Ecamm and StreamYard for our social media video posts. We're doing presentations in front of large groups with videos and PowerPoints (or similar tools) in our VR spaces to create a more memorable and dynamic experience. Video is important, but we believe how we deliver the video viewing experience in the metaverse is what separates us from other firms.

In closing, we're leading with empathy and allowing compassion to serve as our compass when it comes to content and engagement. We've all been through a lot, and the content we create moving forward takes this into consideration.

Mitch Jackson, Esq. aka The Metaverse Lawyer (MetaverseLawyer.io) has spoken twice at Tony Robbins Business Mastery and is a 2013 California Litigation Lawyer of the Year. His popular LinkedIn Newsletter "Metaverse, Web3, Law and Tech" is recommended by Dori Clark, David Meerman Scott and many others.

16. Daniella Malfitano

In this time of The Great Resignation, it is clear that creativity, connection and entrepreneurship is on the rise more now than ever before! I believe that more people will start their own online digital business in 2022 than any other year in history, and that the traditional 9-5 workweek will become almost completely obsolete.

This is a moment of healthy growth and transformation, and in that comes a fresh new approach to productivity and how people want to spend the quality of their everyday lives. What's become clear in this moment of uncertainty, is that we are all seeking something slightly different than our current reality. We all want a better, more improved life, and with enough intention, our collective world can transform into a better vision for our future.

Daniella Malfitano aka Chef "D Malfi" is a multi-faceted entrepreneur, media entertainer, culinary thought leader, health and wellness advocate and classically trained chef. She is a producer, writer, director, set designer and host of several on-stage, online, and televised shows her including her own in-park cooking edutainment family-friendly in-park shows (2016-2020) for The Disney California Adventure® Food & Wine Festival, her online shows "Plant-Based Made Easy" (2020/2021) and "My Choice Kitchen" (2019), and formerly her PBS travel and cooking series "Delicious Discoveries" (2011).

17. Rob Greenlee

We will see more convergence between the video and audio creator communities as the synergies between the two get utilized more to grow audiences faster in Podcasting and YouTube.

We will also see the saturation of global podcast distribution in all active music streaming platforms and then the next phase is the development of new podcast listening apps that focus on appealing to gender, race and genre vertical communities.

We will also see the growth of many full-service podcasting support companies that are helping grow the professionalization of the medium. These fast-growing companies are bringing new compelling podcasters to the medium that would never have done all the needed work to create a podcast and video series. These new creators are likely to have already built communities on their own and that gives them a leg up on growing audience. These services companies create more systematic processes that create efficiencies because of the amount of hard work it takes to be successful and consistently produce, market, distribute, and monetize digital online content.

Rob Greenlee is the VP, Podcast Content & Partnerships at Libsyn.com and Co-Host of NewMediaShow.com. A 17-year podcaster, he was inducted into the Podcasters Hall of Fame in 2017.

18. Nicole Sanchez

Even though in-person events are returning, companies will continue to offer pre-recorded, live-streamed, and VR events as an option for attendees. As a result, the videos' production value, live-streams, and VR events will go up, significantly enhancing the user experience. You'll also see companies heavily repurposing the content from these events across YouTube and other social media platforms.

With sixty-eight percent of consumers preferring to watch videos to learn about new products or services, as compared to articles, infographics, ebooks, and presentations, and eighty-two percent favoring live video over reading social media posts, companies will move to produce more video content than ever before. The video content they create needs to be something that their audience receives value from and wants to watch. Self-promotional, corporate videos won't go far.

High-performing videos need to be engaging, address a need, and tell a story. In the planning stages, before a video is shot, hard questions must be asked. Why will someone want to spend their precious time watching this video? What will they get out of it? How can we serve our viewers/prospects? Since people prefer to get information from people they enjoy watching and trust, the over 13-billion-dollar influencer market will continue to grow as companies continue to partner with influencers to target very specific markets.

Nicole Sanchez is currently a video producer and YouTube strategist for Snowflake and has consulted with tech companies such as Cisco and HPE. Nicole is also an avid live-streamer and YouTube content creator and runs her channel YayOrNayNicole.

19. Andrew Kan

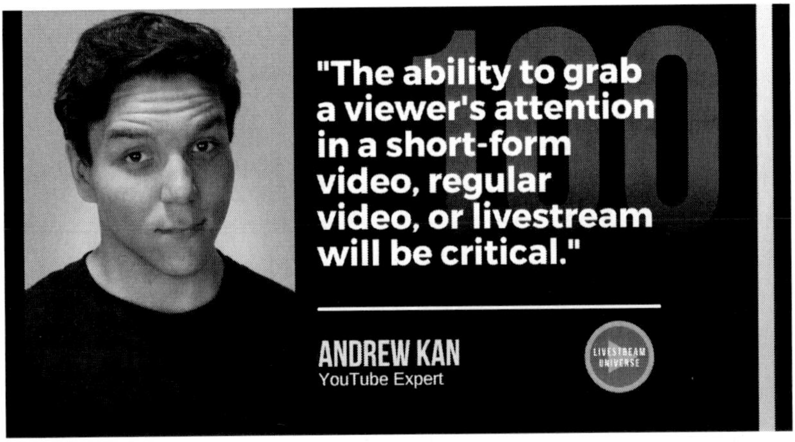

My prediction is that storytelling in all forms will be more important than ever. The ability to grab a viewer's attention in a short-form video (less than one minute), regular video, or livestream will be critical. Finding ways to utilize all three together will be big. The best way to combine all three is to remember the value you want to deliver to your audience, and consistently do that with your content across all three content types.

Andrew Kan is an experienced director in video production with a demonstrated history of working in the computer software industry. Skilled in Storytelling, YouTube Search Engine Optimization (SEO), Customer Relationship Management (CRM), Camera Operation, and Team Building, Andrew is a strong media and communication professional with a Degree focused in Film/Video and Photographic Arts from the Academy of Art University. He used these skills to grow TubeBuddy's YouTube channel from 6,000 to 500,000 subscribers, helped establish the YouTube Strategy for Salesforce Careers &

University YouTube Channel, and teaches over 10,000+ Subscribers how to understand Filmmaking and YouTube on his personal channel.

20. Jessika Phillips

We are currently entering a new world of online – the third wave of the web. The first wave was data, the second was social media and now we're entering the metaverse.

The metaverse is the evolution of how online interactions are taking place. It's the shift towards a co-created, immersive web experience that means that businesses and creators will engage with their communities in new ways.

I believe that it's an exciting time to be both a creator and business owner, as we have an opportunity to think through how to best show up in this evolving space in order to drive engagement and create community.

With that, I think there are 22 core areas that businesses must focus on to be relevant in 2022:

1. **Starting from the Inside Out:** Brands will realize that in order to stand out, they need to create a brand personality

that is reflective of their values. Brands need to understand who they're here to do business with and focus on their culture in order to attract and retain the right teammates and clients. With every hire, a brand is either adding culture credit or debt which means that brands will need to work to establish "Culture Credit" by working with passionate and engaged individuals… people who value time and peace of mind over money… people who want to be inspired. When a brand's team and clients start singing the praises of the organization's culture, THAT is when you know you've hit the nail on the head.

2. **#Unfiltered Brand Communication:** Brands will start to lift the veil between the company and their community. By sharing "Unfiltered" content, being transparent and giving insight into the core of the business, brands will create more conversations with their communities. I believe that brands will become more comfortable communicating with their customers via messenger, text, and social, as it shows a willingness to meet customers where they are at.
3. **Monetization on Messenger:** Brands will look into Messenger Marketing and Automation via chatbots in the inbox to streamline communications. Brands that lean into technology to help facilitate real-time, personalized conversations (by allowing them to start on Messenger and be followed up with a real person) will be brands that grow relationships.
4. **Live Video Selling:** eCommerce brands will wake up to the realization of using live video to engage, answer questions and ultimately sell, in real-time on live video. This is a huge opportunity to build a new pillar of engaged and loyal customers.
5. **Social Audio:** Podcasts, Clubhouse, Twitter Spaces and Facebook's audio functionality will continue to grow via

social AND in the inbox, as a way of creating more individualized and human conversations thanks to the intimacy of audio.

6. **Producing Perfection:** I believe brands will start investing more to amplify the quality and production value of their live videos and micro-content. Similarly, they'll start leaning into producing more short-form content than ever before through hiring producers to help amplify the production value.
7. **Becoming Craveable:** Brands will start to consider leaning into creative ways to incorporate AR/VR apps and figure out how to build this functionality into their brand strategies. This will help customers become more immersed in our brands through the creation of engaging experiences that evoke emotion and tap into the senses.
8. **Emotional Intelligence:** Brands will aim to tap more into emotional intelligence in order to connect with prospective customers and teammates. They will look into more relatable and personalized approaches to marketing communications. I think brands would benefit greatly from incorporating Neurolinguistic Programming into their overall marketing communications strategy.
9. **Co-Creating:** Brands will look at ways of owning the conversation by collecting client data, facilitating client conversations, and building community hubs and apps such as Discord or MightyNetworks.
10. **Brands Within The Brand:** Personal branding is here to stay, and that's a really good thing for brands vs. something to perceive as a threat. Brands will start to embrace hiring, supporting, and showcasing personal brands within their brand in order to expand their business. Many brands will even start to look towards hiring an internal influencer to help grow relationships with their ideal clients.

11. **User-Generated Content:** Brands will focus on ways to let their audience amplify their story by creating moments, opportunities, and rewards for their audience to create and share UGC.
12. **Affiliate links:** With the growth of dark social, brands understand that people trust their friends more than companies, and brands are willing to pay for it. Brands will start to invest more into ways they can actively encourage fans of their brand to share about the brand with their communities.
13. **Analytics:** Brands will focus more on establishing, understanding, and auditing their data to see where, how, and why their community engages. This will help shape where a brand should invest its time, money, and resources.
14. **Strategy:** Brands will recognize that it's less about the tools and more about the technique used. By building better #Hxperiences (human experiences,) customers will feel like VIPS because they've got inside scoop, instant access and on-demand services when, where, and how they want them. It's all about speed and ease of use.
15. **Activation Of Advocates:** Brand marketing will shift internally to reinforce the culture and build a strong foundation so that teams, customers, and communities want to support them. This shift will show that brands understand that their current clients, community, and team members are their most valuable influencers.
16. **Community Creation:** Brands will realize the importance of collaboration and connecting with like-minded brands who have their own built-in, trusted, audiences. Brands will start co-creating content and offers that benefit both of them AND their clients. The focus will be on creating a sense of belonging instead of buying.

17. **Personalized Content:** Brands will lean into the power of personalized videos, emails, audio messages, and ads as a way of providing personalized content. Brands will also invest in tools that will help with data collection to help streamline ways to provide more direct support for clients.
18. **Hybrid Environments:** Brands will consider ways to merge their online and offline communities through events and business processes. They'll look for ways to enhance the online experiences to be more immersive and engaging so that their community stays engaged.
19. **Frictionless and Flexible:** Brands will start looking for ways to create online portals that allow their clients to perform actions that were once only done in person. Similarly, brands will invest in tools that allow for online financing, flexible payment options, and rewards to help take ownership of their buying process.
20. **Cashing in On Clever:** Since the value of our content is in the eyes of our community, brands will start to find new ways to cash in on their clever, edutainment-style content. Because social apps are now allowing for the tipping of creators and creator monetization, plus the shift towards collectors coins and NFTs, brands will recognize that there's a shift towards creators cashing in on clever and see that the value is determined in the eyes of the brand's community.
21. **SoLoMo:** Brands will look towards advancing their social, local, and mobile presence. In order to drive repeat business, brands must go above and beyond their promises. Brands will work harder to grow social proof through reviews and aim to optimize directory listings. Not to mention, brands will need to establish a solid SEO presence if they want to stand out amongst a sea of samesies.
22. **SEO:** Brands will need to rethink SEO over the overall website page experience and Google's Core Updates. Brands

will find ways to turn their website into a high-speed, self-serve, interactive resource hub that gives their visitors a reason to return.

Let's face it – 2020 and 2021 rapidly increased the rate of customer adaptation of fast, self-serve approaches to doing business online.

Customers want speed, accessibility, and convenience, which is why this third web wave – the metaverse – requires a mindset shift around how business is done.

Everything we do should revolve around showing how our brand aligns with our core values and messaging so that we can build and enhance the exceptional experiences of our customers.

It's not a funnel but rather a flywheel approach to marketing and maintaining our brand relationships.

The overall focus for 2022 will be to build relationships in order to turn followers into our biggest fans, our clients into our biggest advocates, our team members into our biggest evangelists, and our community members into collaborators. It's about showing up to relate to our customers on a personal level while operating with a service-over-selling approach.

Doing this will allow us to create organic marketing momentum that attracts, retains, and secures the brand; it serves as a magnet instead of a bullhorn and is truly how we out-care the competition.

Jessika Phillips is an award-winning marketing strategist known for her outspoken dedication to relationship marketing. Jessika helps brands organically build sustainable, craveable, and profitable businesses by out-CARE-ing the competition. Founder of NOW Marketing Group and the Relationship Marketing System. Jessika has been named the go-

to expert on Relationship Marketing & has built a team of 16+ who serve over 100 global brands. Jessika is often asked to share her knowledge and insight as an industry-leading influencer. Jessika also gives back to her community and welcomes 300+ attendees and world-renowned speakers to her Social Media Week Lima conference annually. She is one who leads from the heart to help others love more, give more and be more every day.

21. Dave Jackson

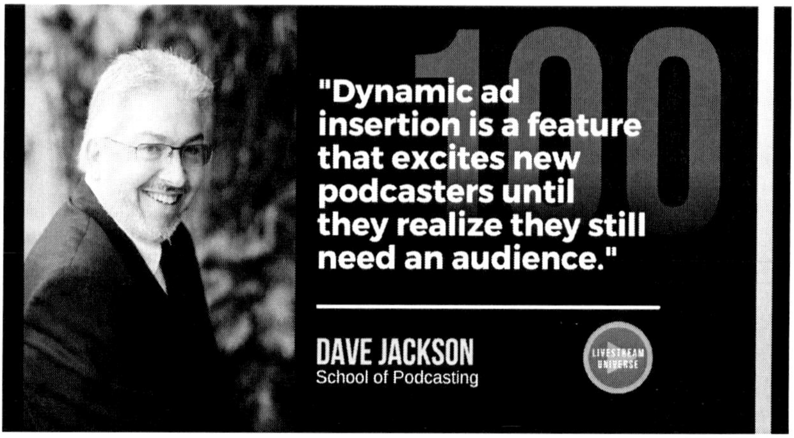

Spotify will continue to build its walled garden. As this is the direct opposite of podcasting's open nature, unless Spotify comes up with a new app that focuses on podcasting, and its celebrities continue to deliver "meh" content, it will do better with new podcast listeners than enticing people currently listening to podcasts to leave their current app. Spotify will also release new exciting features with an asterisk. For example, "YOU CAN PLAY MUSIC IN YOUR PODCAST" (that's only available in this location and only to these people). These sound important and fascinate the uneducated future podcaster.

The Value for Value model of streaming bitcoin to podcasters will continue to grow, but adoption of the technology (both for bitcoin and the new updates to the RSS spec) will be PAINFULLY slow. Frustrated at the pace of adoption (and full of technical know-how) one of those nerds/geeks is going to launch a media host that fully embraces all the technology. While they won't be IAB compliant, nobody will care as the focus won't be on advertising. It will be the revenge of the nerds. Sales of "How you like me now?" T-shirts will fly off the shelves.

A large portion of the shows that started in March of 2020 during the pandemic will cease production as they are neither rich nor famous.

Every life coach will now add "podcast consultant" to their title.

New services will launch with promises of growing your podcast audience. There will be no videos. There will be no about page. There will be no explanation. All you need to do is provide your email address and they will explain it to you. Yes, people will still fall for that.

Dynamic ad insertion will be the feature that media hosts will be adding if they haven't already. This excites new podcasters until they realize they still need an audience.

Amazon (realizing that Apple wakes up about twice a year to hit podcastsconnect.apple.com much like Fonzi hitting the jukebox to make sure its working in the TV show Happy Days) will take steps to get more of the market. They will also try the "Exclusive" route of content by offering deals to celebrities. This exclusive – only available on Amazon – content will become available everywhere after about six months and they realize that people want to listen where they want to listen.

Hardware companies will launch more recorders, microphones, etc with the podcaster in mind.

iHeart radio will be Number 1 at saying they are number 1. I believe they also invented air.

Figuring that "It's better than a poke in the eye" podcasters will accept lower advertising rates (and completely ignore the value of their audience) so they can buy that can of Mountain Dew at the end of the month (if it goes on sale).

4000 "Interesting shows featuring interesting people telling interesting stories" will be launched on 1/1/22.

Dave Jackson is the founder of the School of Podcasting where he has been helping people plan, launch, grow and monetize their podcast since 2005.

22. Nancy Ancowitz

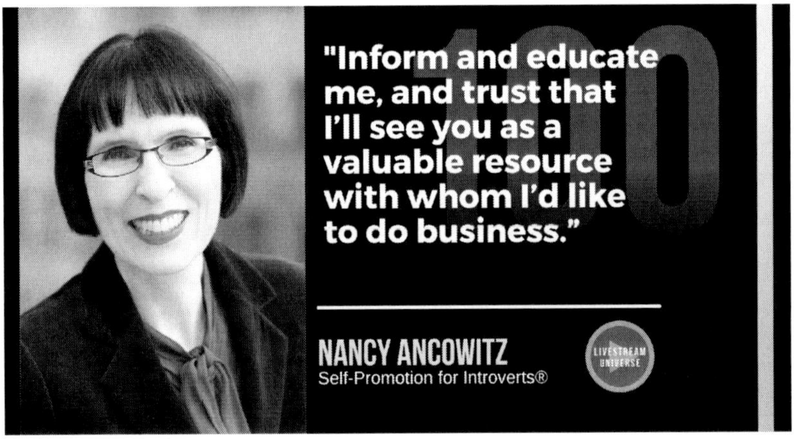

I predict—okay, at least hope—that content creators won't try to tell everything they know about a topic. Instead, I'm hoping they create content with a few big ideas (at a time, anyhow!). To the extent possible, let those big ideas put me at the hub of the wheel, so I can take them in a direction that I find useful. Speaking of that direction, I always like to shop for information and draw my own conclusions, rather than being "sold to." Inform and educate me, and trust that I'll see you as a valuable resource with whom I'd like to do business.

Also, since you're always interested in how to make content introvert-friendly, a few tips: 1) give us time to digest the information you share; 2) offer to follow up with valuable information—and then do so; and 3) when you bring us together, remember that we prefer small gatherings, even in a virtual space, to large ones. Lastly, we're all complex human beings and "one size fits all" doesn't even work when you're selling socks.

Nancy Ancowitz is a coach specializing in career advancement and presentation skills, an NYU adjunct professor and the author of "Self-Promotion for Introverts®: The Quiet Guide to Getting Ahead." She blogs for Psychology Today and used to blog for Salary.com.

23. Jan Koch

Of course I'm biased and think that virtual events will stay and even grow. They're just a fantastic way to demonstrate thought leadership and after being established in the marketing space, I see more and more companies outside the usual marketing industry tap into virtual events.

Other than that, I think that short-form video will dominate. It works extremely well already to build a brand and stay visible in front of your audience. TikTok won't go anywhere and YouTube seems to be pushing Shorts. Combine that with the ever-shortening attention span and you've got the perfect storm for short-form video. The perfect medium to show a little insight into your personality without being too difficult to create.

Jan Koch is the owner of Virtual Summit Mastery and a passionate virtual summit host, connecting with people and building an audience globally. He has been organizing summits since 2015 and brought together well over 15k attendees from 110+ countries on his summits.

24. DAN CURRIER

As the creator economy continues to develop, more organizations will look to follow Amazon's lead and integrate native video into their platforms. This will open up new opportunities for those with the skills to make quality content. Never has there been a better time to learn these skills and/or develop existing skills.

YouTube will remain the leading platform upon which inspiring creators may develop a well-rounded skill set to open these and many other opportunities. The development of the creator economy will empower creators to weigh the exchange of time for money with a newfound appreciation for balance and allow them to create their freedom on their own terms.

Dan Currier is the founder of the People of Video Conference and also runs a successful YouTube channel, Creator Fundamentals, which helps creator build revenue around their content. He also offers a course, Influencer100x.com, that shows creators how to leverage Amazon Influencer video to make thousands a month.

25. Chetachi Egwu Ph.D.

Over the last two years, the pandemic has made video and livestreaming a necessity rather than an option. The streaming universe is now filled with creators, which is excellent. People have realized the value of going live directly to their audiences. However, this also means that there is an overabundance of content, with some of the more popular creators getting the shine.

Thus, my prediction is twofold: More creators will be looking toward apps that serve niche audiences in order to get more attention for their content. Also, creators will look to new places to put content – like the metaverse.

At this point, not only is metaverse a buzzword, but it's also an untapped virtual space that can potentially garner more attention for creators squeezed out of traditional digital spaces. It also offers the potential for creators to be compensated in sought-after cryptocurrencies.

Chetachi Egwu Ph.D. a.k.a. Dr. Tachi is a media professor, filmmaker, media content producer and journalist passionate about media, tech and pop culture. She is currently the host and creator of the live streamed show MediaScope, 1/2 of the TV Twins on the TV channeling podcast, and producer/director of Florida Memorial University's The Lions' Den live stream.

26. Chris Krimitsos

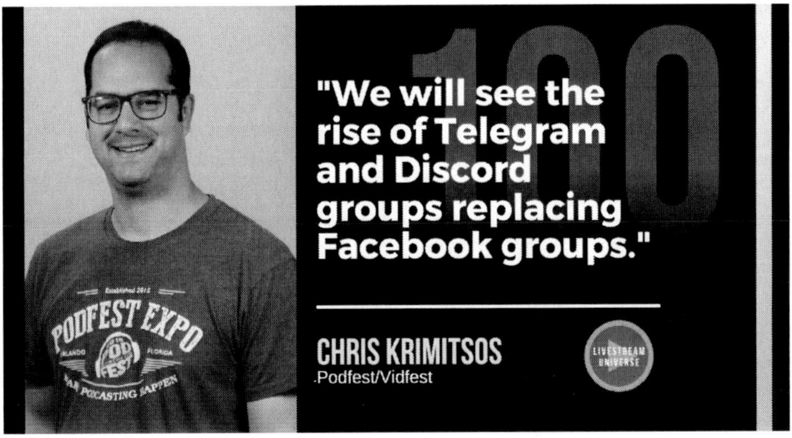

We will see the rise of Telegram and Discord groups replacing Facebook groups. We will see Bitcoin Lightning payments come from the audience to their favorite creator as well. We will also see creators create larger tight-knit communities that they control as well as more premium offerings to their listeners.

Chris Krimitsos is the founder of the Podfest/Vidfest conferences and author of "Start Ugly."

27. Rose Horowitz

If there's a silver lining to our post-pandemic lives, it's that people are communicating in ways that would have been cutting edge just two years ago. The technology existed but from demand springs genius.

Analysts have said the rate of growth in livestreaming viewership started to decline in 2021 compared to 2020. But the industry as a whole has increased by an average of 49 percent in 2021 compared to 2020, according to Stream Hatchet.

Take social audio: it's just getting started. "This allows us to be ourselves in public in a way that I never knew before in social media. I know everybody's personality by one word of their voice." -Overhead in a Twitter Spaces room opening a bid for NFT art.

"Sometimes, 280 characters does not cut it. Sometimes, tweeting isn't the right way of communicating at that moment," Twitter product designer Maya Gold Patterson said when the platform's Audio Spaces was introduced. "Hearing the empathy, emotion and nuance in someone's voice can help people connect at different levels."

For example, I often listen to #TwitterSpaces audio chats as I take walks or respond to emails on my desktop. There's a kind of beauty there. Plus, there are some great surprises. One day, I listened to poetry and music and how they are paired with art for an NFT offering. How cool is that?

I predict that within a year, there will be hybrid versions of social audio with multiple hosts. So, people will be able to go strictly audio or join a livestream to participate in the same conversation. The benefit? Livestreams paired with evolving technology will allow hosts to easily share information and bring in speakers on video while simultaneously running a social audio chat.

Hybrid events are here to stay. Businesses see the benefits of both significantly cutting their costs and reaching a far wider audience.

Best content will continue to be Queen.

In social audio, some platforms are offering incentives to entice the best creators to host and conceive the topics.

Twitter seems to be ahead in a few ways. With its Communities feature, Twitter is encouraging creators to be more engaged. Users can join these new social hubs and tweet to other people with shared interests rather than their wider group of followers.

In another initiative launched in the fall, Twitter's Spark program is paying selected creators $2,500 a month for three months to host at least two audio shows a week. The selected participants will also get ad credits and Spaces swag.

It's a smart move: sustaining audience interest in new media hinges on more than attracting top minds in technology. It needs experienced, innovative creators who know not only how to create great content but how to deliver it.

Rose Horowitz is a Pulitzer-nominated journalist who is the founder of #WomenToFollow, a global hashtag trend that had a reach of 12 million views in its first two weeks. She's a thought leader on women's issues, a content creator, social media pro, livestream producer, and the host of her new livestream "WomenToFollow" show.

28. Tim McDonald

As more hybrid events emerge in 2022, we will see technology providers try to eliminate the pause it takes people on livestreaming to engage vs. an in-person audience member. It has been an ongoing issue since the early days of livestreaming that there are long awkward pauses or talking over people while trying to communicate.

While many hosts have found ways to help eliminate this, the technology providers will begin to assist by improving technology and adding more features that help virtual attendees feel as comfortable with speaking up as in-person attendees.

Tim McDonald is the host of The Business of Speaking, a Stage 4 Colon Cancer Survivor and former Director of Community at Huffington Post. He's the Purveyor of Purpose at Creating Is LLC.

29. Shelly Saves the Day

2022 will see the rise and mass adoption of video podcasting. The ultimate repurposing tool lives in the form of a video podcast. Distribute with video on platforms like YouTube and Anchor/Spotify integration. Audio only streams on all usual platforms for podcast distribution. Audio snippets for audiograms. Quotable graphics from content and blog posts with embedded episodes and show notes. Integrations for creator negotiated product sponsorship posts. Snippets and shorter videos as highlights across all platforms vertical and landscape.

Second prediction will be the rise of shoppable video and video streaming across platforms like Amazon, YouTube, Facebook (Meta) and Instagram.

Shelly Saves the Day is a Seattle-based content creator and founder of iMovie Made Easy, a course designed to help anyone learn how to create video using iMovie to share what they love with the world.

30. ERIC HUNLEY

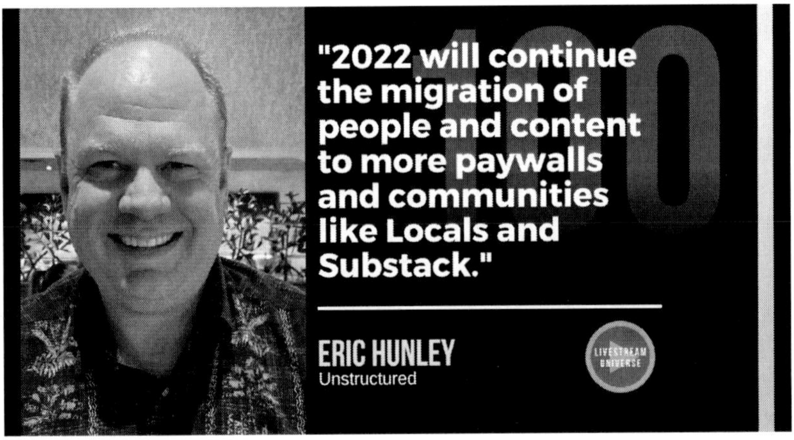

I think that 2022 will continue the migration of people and content to more paywalls and communities like Locals and Substack. With YouTube, Facebook/Instagram, and Twitter constantly either blocking, embellishing or banning content and people, folks are looking for safety and free speech. This has led to an exodus of people going to alternate platforms such as Substack, Locals, and Rumble with the latter two merging and audiences are starting to support creators more directly now through subscriptions and more.

As such, I think the advertising model which has carried the industries is weakening and we are seeing more of a direct democratization of content. The consumers are starting to vote with their dollars directly and this is a great thing.

Eric Hunley is the host of Unstructured and the eponymous YouTube Channel Eric Hunley where he interviews a WIDE variety of folks from body language experts, to YouTube lawyers, to folks in 3 letter agencies.

He also has America's Untold Stories with Eric Hunley and Mark Groubert which explores history and pop-culture that is often unknown, obscure, or overlooked.

31. MICHELLE LEVITT

2021 certainly strengthened the need for online content. I think 2022 will see an even bigger increase across the board. We have all been doing this long enough that people no longer want basic or "phoned-in" online content. I predict 2022 will be the year of the upgrade… better content and better gear! It's no longer "cute" when your dog is barking in your live stream.

Michelle Levitt has been a musician, an artist, and the CEO of her own podcast studio. She's also been the Marketing Director for Heil Sound for the last 17 years.

32. Shamir Allibhai

I predict applications using blockchains/crypto will ultimately be where most creators spend their energies and 2022 will see a lot more creators getting exposed to this frontier. In 2022, Tik Tok usage will continue to explode and creators will continue to gravitate to it, but they will find it is harder to rise above the noise as the platform gets saturated. There's one view that as Covid gets under control we'll see a return to in-person events: I think virtual events will grow 10x!

Shamir Allibhai is a builder of video tech. He's the founder of collaborative video editor in the browser, Simon Says.

33. Super Joe Pardo

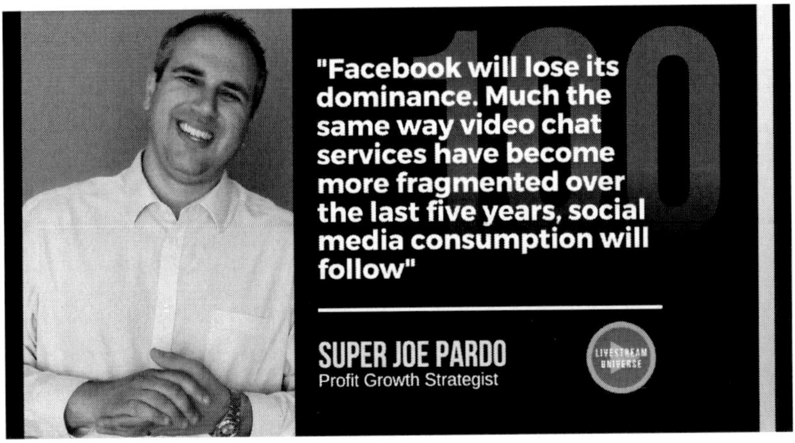

Facebook will lose its dominance in the social media arena. The outage of 2021 is foreshadowing what is to come for the giant. Much the same way video chat services have become more fragmented over the last five years, social media consumption will follow.

A Profit Strategist, "Super" Joe Pardo brings a series of strategy, application, and execution planning to every entrepreneur, team, or business that he works with. Founder of The Super Joe Pardo Show on YouTube and the Independent Podcast Conference, Joe focuses on putting the right methods into the best practices in order to bring about personalized solutions for each client.

34. TERRY JOHNSON

We will see an increase in using artificial intelligence (AI) technologies to effortlessly create relevant content that will attract your target audience online. More creators will use AI tools and machine learning to deliver tailored messages to the right audience at the right time. These tools will be available for users in current and future apps.

Terry Johnson is a digital marketing strategist and consultant with a background in advertising, marketing and tech. She is the host of "This Week's Marketing Chat", a weekly, live stream with topics on marketing strategy and social media for small businesses at terryjohnsononline.live.

35. Jim Harold

2022 will see more IRL streams via mobile. As phones, connectivity and apps improve, IRL mobile streams will account for a greater percentage of total live streams as we get out from behind our desks and take our viewers with us!

Jim Harold is a professional podcaster at Jim Harold Media LLC with more than 50 million downloads. He hosts The Paranormal Podcast® and Jim Harold's Campfire, which are among the Top 1% most downloaded podcasts on the industry's largest podcast host, Libsyn. Jim's also the executive producer of Unpleasant Dreams and the author of five volumes of "Jim Harold's Campfire: True Ghost Stories" (All Kindle #1 Supernatural Best Sellers).

36. Meiko Patton

Social audio will continue to dominate in 2022. There are many clones, but Clubhouse will continue to be the leader if they continue to innovate and remain true to their vision. Audio unlike any other medium draws the listener in. A person can form a connection within seconds. I see the emergence of audio NFT's and a way for Web 3.0 to include audio. Social audio will also play a role in the rise of cryptocurrency and creator-generated coins.

Meiko Patton helps PR Firms effortlessly increase their revenue by leveraging Clubhouse by using her Proprietary ClubMetrics Framework.

37. Brenden Mulligan

In 2022, the audio format will continue to grow exponentially across podcasting and live experiences (Twitter Spaces / Clubhouse).

Creators will focus on creating tight-knit communities where they have a direct connection with their audience, using podcast players as a distribution channel to draw listeners into a more intimate connection.

Twitter Spaces and Clubhouse will find its way into the traditional podcasting distribution channels.

Brenden Mulligan is the creator of Podpage, a podcast website platform used by over 10,000 podcasters to create instant, self-updating, gorgeous podcast websites.

38. Joie Gharrity

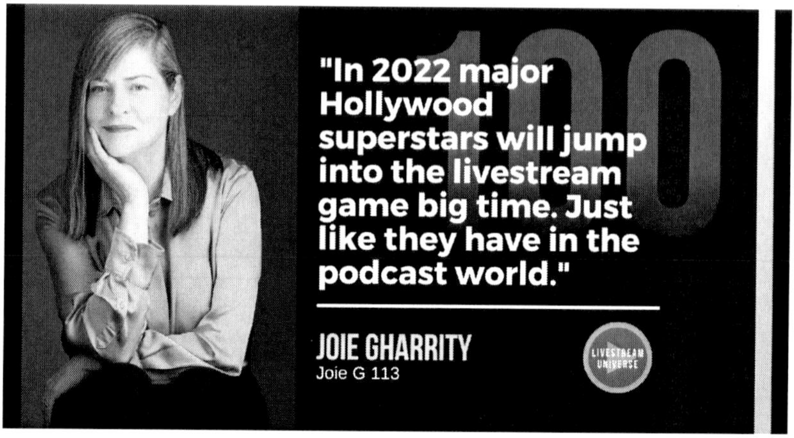

In 2022 major Hollywood superstars will jump into the livestream game big time. Just like they have in the podcast world.

Joie Gharrity is the founder of Joie G 113. An author and international speaker, she worked in the Hollywood entertainment industry for 15+ years at top companies in film, television, original web content, and branded entertainment.

39. S. Chris Edmonds

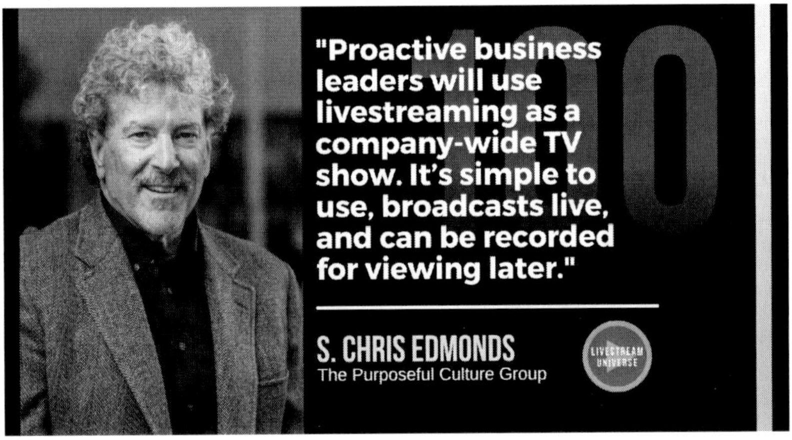

This coming year, proactive business leaders will use livestreaming as a company-wide TV show. It's simple (as simple as Zoom) to use; it broadcasts live; and livestreams can be recorded for viewing later. Effective leaders communicate proactively and frequently to educate players about company performance, company events, service/volunteer opportunities & impact, upcoming transitions or changes in the business, and more.

In addition, livestreaming lets leaders respond to questions from viewers live (via chat) or through pre-submitted questions. These broadcasts need to occur weekly on a regular schedule. The difference between livestreaming and video meetings like Zoom? Viewers aren't required to be on screen; it's less demanding on viewers, makes for a simpler screen/presentation, and puts the messaging and the messenger front and center.

S. Chris Edmonds is a speaker, author, executive consultant, and president & CEO of The Purposeful Culture Group.

He's published three Amazon bestselling books, the latest being "Good Comes First," co-authored with Mark S. Babbitt to help senior leaders create uncompromising work cultures where respect is as important as results.

40. Jennie Mustafa-Julock

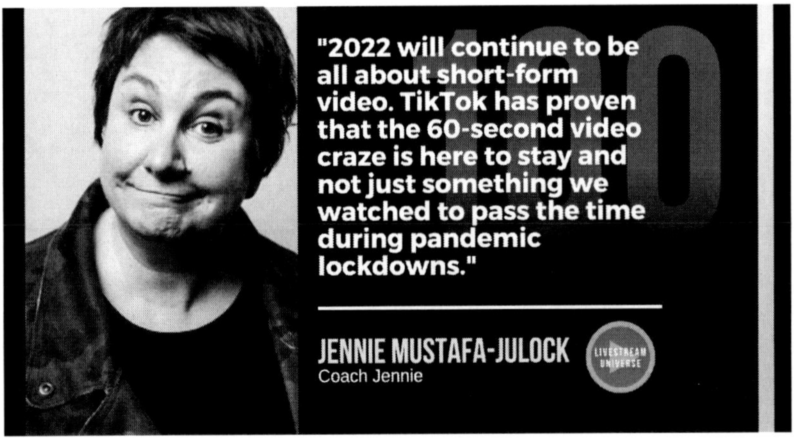

At the risk of sounding like Captain Obvious, I predict that 2022 will continue to be all about short-form video. TikTok has proven that the 60-second video craze is here to stay and not just something we watched to pass the time during pandemic lockdowns. I'm particularly eager to see how YouTube will prioritize Shorts for channel growth as its response to TikTok's popularity – especially for video creators who provide substantive intellectual value without silly dance moves. Hopefully, this will encourage more creators to create more 60-second videos that matter. But sadly, I also predict that the ridiculously-embarrassing-pointing-at-word-bubbles trend is not going to end anytime soon. (sigh)

Jennie Mustafa-Julock is Coach Jennie, an inner critic expert helping clients get out of their own way so they can get on with the business of changing the world. She's the author of "Hilda: Tackle Your Inner Naysayer, Get Out of Your Own Way, and Unleash Your Badassery."

41. Professor Nez

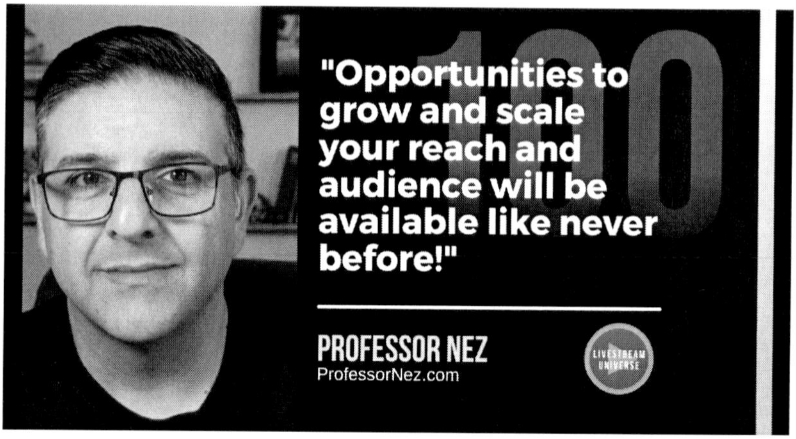

The Live-streaming Wars are going to heat up in 2022 between big platforms like YouTube, Facebook, Twitch, TikTok and more. This is a huge gift for creators and brands as more opportunities to grow and scale your reach and audience will be available like never before!

Professor Nez is a content creator, business owner and real-world educator with over four million views across multiple channels and mediums including live-streaming, VOD (Video on Demand) short-form content and more.

42. Nancy Myrland

For 2022, I am seeing a few new developments and approaches in content, social, and digital. The name of the game is personal. Our marketing efforts need to revolve around developing personal relationships with those we care about. Anyone can market the umbrella firm and its products and services, but our clients want to see who and what we are made of. They need to know there are real, caring people behind the name.

To accomplish this, and to help our profiles come to life, I am still extremely bullish on voice and video, and think firms and companies need to develop sound strategies in these areas. Voice and video will help them stand out from those who are not willing to take the time to figure it out, but perhaps even more important is that voice and video accelerate the personal approach I talked about a moment ago. Video doesn't have to be professionally produced these days. It can be, but situational video that comes across as more personal and is a glimpse of the person helps the viewer understand what you might be like to do business. Regarding audio, I'd like to see my clients continue to adopt podcasting as a way to share expertise and to develop relationships with those trusting enough to place them in their ears for a dedicated amount of time. What a gift that is.

Let's talk about LinkedIn. We also need to continue to pay strong attention to LinkedIn. It is maturing and evolving from the gentle giant I have always known, into a gentle, professional giant that has its head down, focusing on innovation, knowing when to innovate and when to pull back on features that don't work. They are doubling down on what creators and consumers are craving, which is knowledge and content in different formats that will help them become smarter and more valuable in their individual companies and communities. I have seen an amazing and appreciated uptick in LinkedIn training requests, and I expect that to continue for at least the next few years while LinkedIn continues to come into its own, and while my professionals realize its importance in building their reputations and relationships.

Nancy Myrland is a marketing and business development advisor, specializing in content, social, and digital media marketing for business lawyers and their legal marketers. She does LinkedIn training (including her first online course: LinkedInCourseForLawyers.com), works with firms on launching podcasts, polishing their virtual presentation skills, learning video and livestreaming skills, blogging, social media (obviously), and hosts two podcasts.

43. Larry Roberts

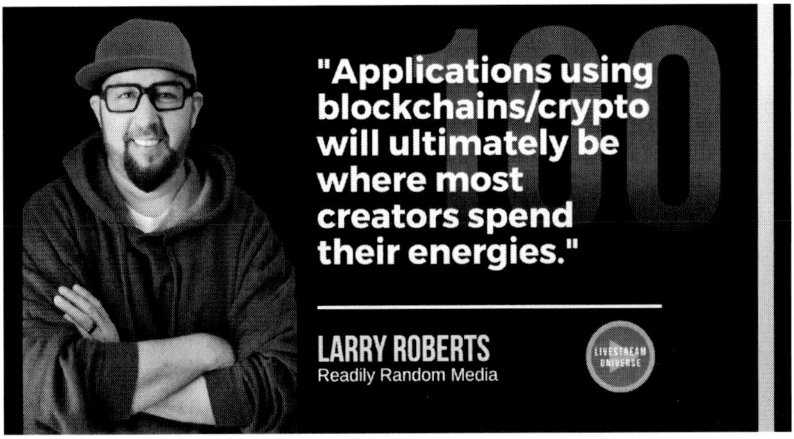

I predict that video content in a variety of formats will continue to grow and play a critical role in the success of content creators. If we look at where we are at today, podcasters continue to find bigger audiences with the inclusion of video, email marketing is embedding short videos in their content and if you look at platforms like Firesides Chat, you'll see social audio is including video as well. For further proof, look at the success and impact that Reels are having on Instagram.

Even a creator with a minimal following can still generate thousands of views for a Reel, with the vast majority of the views coming from non-followers. Where else can you get that level of engagement and all of the demographic-specific data behind it? Good luck getting that level of detail with audio-only. This isn't to say that podcasting and audio-only aren't still major players in the content space, but without video, I believe that ever-elusive audience engagement will be more and more difficult to find for the indie creator.

Larry Roberts is a high energy and charismatic podcaster, speaker, best selling author and international top rated course creator with over 1000 students in 51 countries. Featured in Podcast Magazine (April 2020) Larry is the Editor in Chief of The Podfest Messenger, one of the largest podcast industry newsletters and regularly publishes articles in various podcast periodicals, he appears on other podcasts and can be found speaking at industry events.

44. Bridgetti Lim Banda

My prediction is that the upward trajectory we are seeing in livestreaming is not going to slow down any time soon. In fact, it's going to speed up and simply become as natural as the air that we breathe. One of the areas in which I see the biggest growth taking place is livestreamed shopping. It's an entertaining and interactive customer shopping experience that helps customers add items to their shopping cart. Much like the trusted in-store promoters who helped us make in-person buying choices, livestreamed ecommerce is a shopping experience and will become the QVC 2.0 interactive shopping experience on steroids. It's going to disrupt the supply chain ecosystem.

Never before have we had the technology and reach that allows for a three-dimensional shopping experience with an online sales associate being able to interface with clients around the globe in real-time. With relationship marketing brands can get products and services their customers want to market faster and cheaper.

Bridgetti Lim Banda helps business owners incorporate live video into their marketing strategy. She's a Livestream Producer, Talk Show Host, Global Goodwill Ambassador and most recently accomplished becoming a two-time #1 Best-Selling Amazon collaborative anthology author.

45. STEVEN GREENE

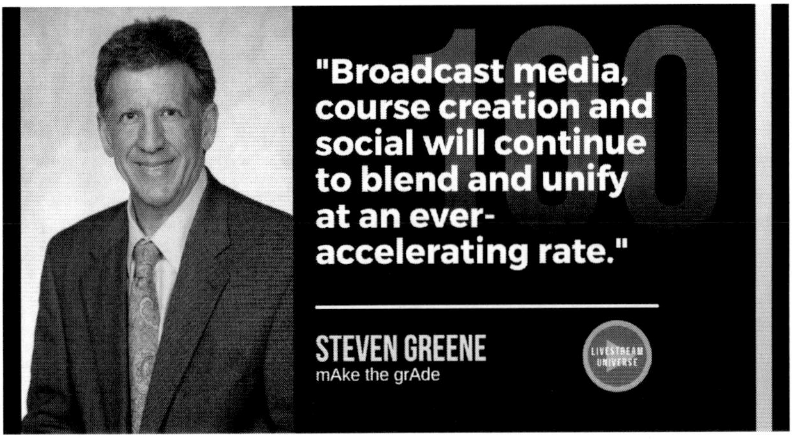

The amalgam of broadcast media, course creation and social will continue to blend and unify at an ever-accelerating rate. "Solomediaists" (yes I have coined that term Ross Brand – or is "solomediaers" better?) (those who produce only one type of content output) will become rarer while "multimediaists" – those who can produce content and project into a myriad of platforms will thrive. This process is driven by the expansion of technology which enables the production of these media.

Dr. Steven Greene is an educator, best-selling author and multimediaist focused on education and making the world a better place.

46. CAREN GLASSER

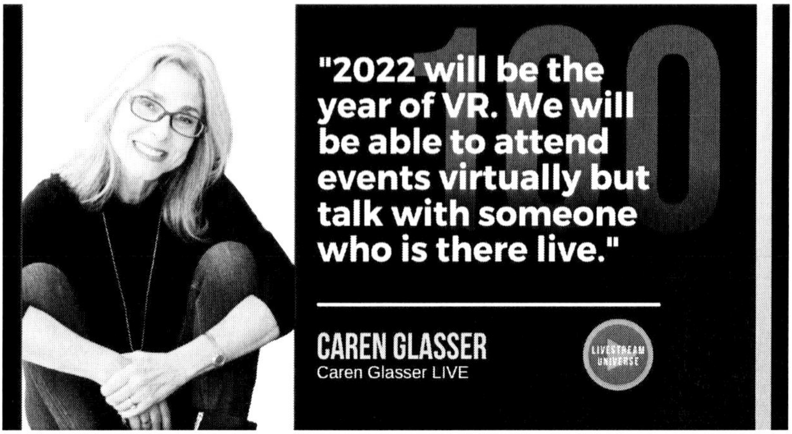

2022 will be the year of VR (Virtual Reality). Live events and VR events will come together to bring a hands-on experience to attendees no matter how they are attending; Live or Virtually. Desktop/Laptop/iPad/Mobile navigation in the VR space will become easier to use meaning there will be no barrier to entry. Networking events will never be the same as we will be able to attend virtually but still be able to talk with someone who is there live. The possibilities are endless…. and I'm all in!

Caren Glasser is the Producer of five online talk shows and hosts four of her own talk shows. In addition, she is in production for a new kind of event: VR networking launching in January 2022.

47. KEVIN KOLBE

I predict we'll see Apple launch a Facebook-type alternative to finally compete in the social media space. Combine their many Mac offerings that make it easy for creators to create plus appeal to Mac-only lovers, then combine that with privacy issues and such and you could have a formidable new social media experience.

Kevin Kolbe is a content creator and video coach. He helps creators create, do more with video, share their gifts, and make an impact in the world.

48. Anita Sonya

Livestreaming becomes a must for personal branding. It will continue to grow in 2022 even as in-person events start happening again.The pandemic has pushed people all over the world to make money online. It does not matter if you know about technology or not. You know you have to survive before being able to thrive.

It can be difficult at first for people living in developing countries since it is not only about the cost (and the requirement to pay in USD), but also the quality of the internet connections you can get. If livestreaming platforms and social media want to grow in developing Asia-Pacific markets, they need to change some policies to make it easier for end-users in those countries.

Even with these challenges, there are great opportunities to connect and communicate with people all over the world. Those benefits of livestreaming helped me host three virtual events, grow my business and even land a big brand sponsor like Restream.

Livestreaming is important not only for coaches, trainers, speakers and artists who need to boost their visibility, but for retailers in live e-commerce. People make decisions to shop from the livestreams created by the sellers and can order right away on the platform before moving to payment. Local online marketplaces support those features to influence buyers, but you still need to build your own community so the customer comes to you.

Let's say livestreaming never dies… just like her soulmate, the podcast. They complete each other.

Anita Sonya is the founder of Livestream Your Brand. She helps business owners transform their businesses through livestreaming and online events. She hosts multiple international virtual summits each year, bringing together top speakers from diverse industries, and is planning her first internatiional in-person event for 2023 in Bali.

49. Chris Strub

Direct monetization options for individual creators will continue to expand and evolve, making the influencer market even more expensive and difficult to navigate for big brands. In turn, these self-sustaining creators will yield even more power to influence brands, as audiences' loyalty will continue to shift from venerable brands to recognizable individuals. Brand partnerships will inevitably become less well-defined, as legal lines get blurred by deeper product integrations and cleverly undisclosed marketing approaches.

As the 'Giving Day Guy,' Chris Strub produces and co-hosts live-streamed fundraising events around the country. Chris is the first person to live-stream in all 50 states and the author of the new book, "Fifteen Seconds of Fame," about the proliferation of Instagram Stories.

50. Kyle Bondo

The Coming Upheaval: Once upon a time you and your friends could buy some microphones and start a podcast for pennies. Then one of you thought it would be cool if you could get paid to podcast. At that moment the professional podcaster was born. Like all other professions, there are many levels of mastery. Podcasting is no different. Beginners sound like beginners while experts sound like experts. The difference is in the quality.

Producing 800 episodes can make you and your show better. And next year that difference will make ALL the difference in whether or not a listener notices your efforts. To hammer home this vision, I see three emerging trends that will make a seismic shift in podcasting in the waning days of the Pandemic: The Great Podcast Drought, The Rise of Podcasting as Prototype, and The Next Content War.

The Great Podcast Drought: First, tons (a real unit of podcasting measurement) of active podcasts will DIE and the number of ACTIVE podcasts on Apple Podcasts will fall BELOW 100,000 as the Content Wars put more and more active podcasts behind paywalls. Paywalls WILL make 1 in 10 podcaster's wealthy, however, for every podcast that generates revenue there will be nine others that do not.

The Rise of Podcasting as Prototype: Next, Hollywood will use podcasting to continue to prototype new TV and Movie content creating a whole cadre of podcasters who become showrunners, writers, and producers for REAL production companies. Additionally, these podcasts will feature a tidal wave of known A/B/C level actors. Podcasts like The Oyster and Black Box are already proving this.

The Next Content War: Finally, The Content Wars heat up as media companies start buying up podcasters, podcast networks, podcast content, or any audio content not nailed down or copyrighted. This is when the giant named Apple will finally awaken from its sleep. Brought on by its new CEO who sees podcasting as an important part of their platform for the first time since Steve Jobs. Because of this realization, Apple will start hosting podcast content and threaten indy podcast hosting companies. This will cause indy podcast companies to start buying out their competitors to form bigger hosting monsters and see the rise of new podcast hosting companies appearing to support podcasts that have been kicked off of bigger platforms. As one market shrinks another will be born.

I think each of these areas impacts the future of podcasting in one fundamental way: the industry will dramatically change to reduce the friction in starting and monetizing a QUALITY podcast. If you fine-tune your profession by increasing the quality of your podcast, you might be one of those podcasts that survive the coming upheaval. Have no fear my friends – I strongly believe that quality finally gets rewarded in 2022!

Kyle Bondo is the Chief Creative and Co-Founder of a podcast production company (gagglepod.com) that specializes in audio experience (AX) design from story/content development to audio editing and publication.

51. Tina VaLant

Podcasting enjoys an incredible boost, as livestream creators forage new frontiers, repurposing audio from videos and lives, into this on-the-go format. Not everyone wants to be on-camera and this satisfies a broad audience, with endless possibilities. OTT media services flourish benefitting their subscribers with instant access and an array of choices to fit every need.

Savvy individuals, organizations, businesses, companies, musical/visual artists will capitalize on the value of direct interaction (via livestream and social media) with commentors, fans/followers, enabling conversion into subscribers, friends, brand influencers, customers/clients and more.

#ServeShareShine is Tina VaLant's motto. She serves as a speaker, photographer, columnist, livestreamer; sharing her talent and enabling others to shine.

52. MIKE WILKERSON

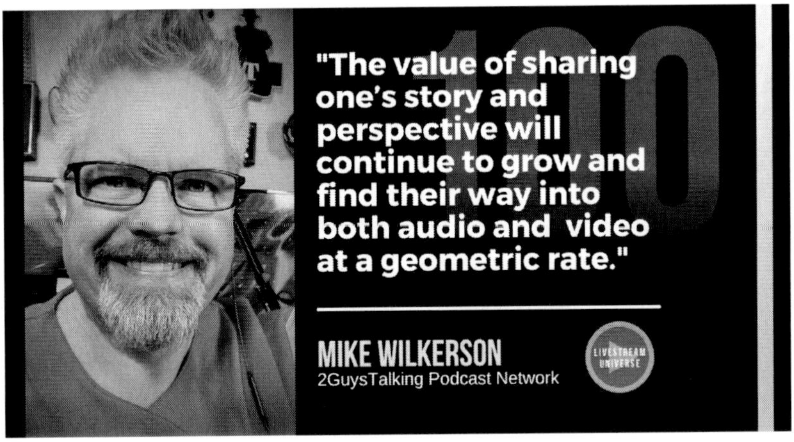

The value of sharing one's story and perspective via their unique experiences and skill sets will continue to grow and find their way into both audio and (when a viable topic) video at a geometric rate. Those who wield these stories and skill sets will finally begin to understand that their life and knowledge are currently a resource that will disappear – the instant that they do, unless they take the time to somehow document it.

If you thought that writing in a diary with a pen was valuable back in the day, then you're guaranteed to finally have one of the most important "lightbulb moments" ever: as you understand why being able to hear, see, experience and learn those from those who go before us is so vital. Their stories, their skill sets, their perspectives – they are LIFE, and they fuel those whom they leave behind. Life finds a way as always because Podcasting is Captured (Life) Perspective.

Mike Wilkerson is an OG Podcaster in St. Louis area, and has crafted, hosted, produced and promoted podcasts of every kind since 2005. His growing Podcast-service-based empire includes a voiceover academy and service (The Voice Farm), a podcast editing academy and service (The Editor Corps) and a program promotion engine (The Podcaster Matrix). He has created 4 retail-based Podcast Studios to capture content to propel each vein of his business. A 5th studio, is the unique and mobile "Podcast Bug" – a 1974 custom Super Beetle with a recording studio built into the front of it. Mike and his always-growing library of programming can be found at 2GuysTalking.Com.

53. Amy Woods

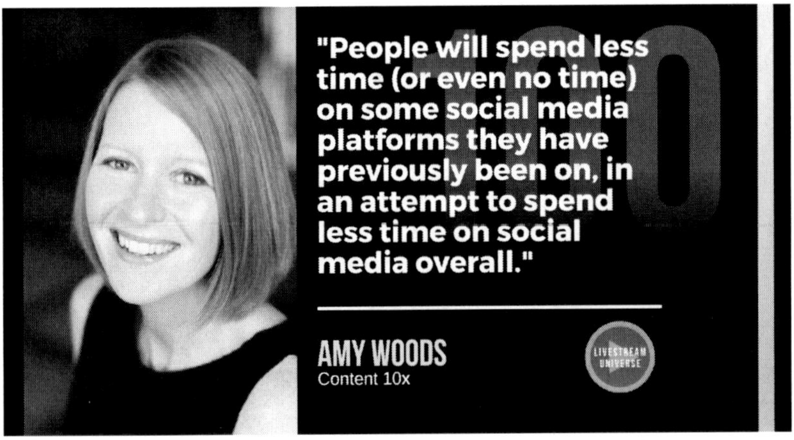

I think people will start to spend less time (or even no time) on some social media platforms they have previously been on, in an attempt to spend less time on social media overall. In doing so, they want to have a more positive experience when they are on social media. They are looking for platform-specific content, and more personalized interactions too, and I think more marketers are going to make both of those a high priority.

Amy Woods is the CEO and founder of Content 10x – a content repurposing agency. Amy and her team work with businesses and brands from all over the world repurposing their content, helping them to reach and impact more people whilst saving them time.

54. Brian Schulman

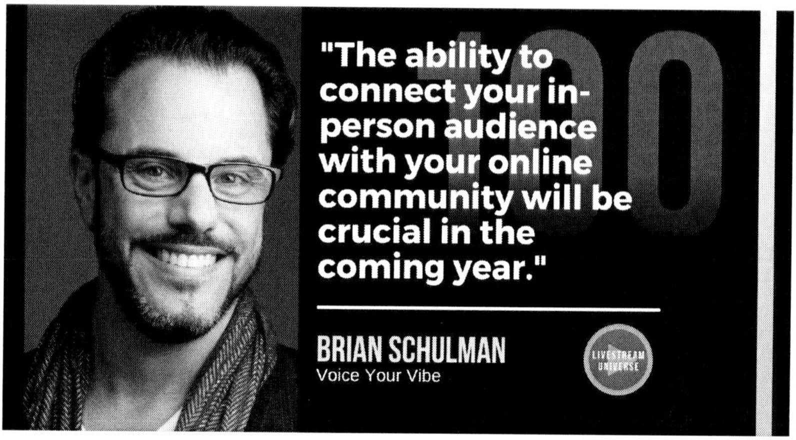

In 2022, people will be creating more relatable, heart-centered, engaging, and compelling live-stream and digital media content targeting wider audiences. The days of showing up one way and acting another are gone. Authenticity is no longer optional, nor is there a choice to wear it as a 'mask'. How sincere/genuine you are will define the success or failure of your show, your brand and business. Humans do want to connect with humans.

We have spent the last 18 months during a global pandemic, digitally, in each other's homes. It is no longer 'business is business' and 'personal is personal'. Showing up professionally has been redefined. Lines blurred. Boundaries shifted. Livestreams are taking on current issues, engaging in discussions that tackle relatable issues and digital media content is no longer all about the 'hard sell'. This trend will continue to grow because it is what people are looking to engage with. They are seeking out spaces, communities and businesses in which they can be themselves.

In 2022, getting real, relatable, having more fun, and being human with your live-stream and digital media content will be key. Furthermore, it is becoming easier and easier to create live-stream and digital media content. This is in part due to 'startup obstacles' that traditionally hindered a quick-start in the past, having been removed. Less capital is required to start, because of the now widely used and accepted virtual space to 'show up' in. Equipment and services are readily accessible and have become more affordable, moreover, the understanding and the ability to use what is already in your hand, (think cell phone and camera/laptop), is the norm and no longer the exception. In fact, you probably already possess the necessary technology to stream live, generate web content, and create digital assets.

Before 2020, people, businesses and entities did not concern themselves with showing up virtually or making content available through a hybrid model, but in 2022 virtual and hybrid events will be in demand. The 'digital space' has opened events to people and communities that may not have ever before had the ability or opportunity to participate and engage with content. In the event arena, what was 'nice to have' prior to the pandemic (a digital component/presence) has shifted to 'must have'. The ability to connect your in-person audience with your online community will be crucial in the coming year. This is where having everything you need in the palm of your hand, both to create and consume live-streaming, web-based content and digital media come together.

Brian Schulman, a 2X best-selling Author, is an International Keynote Speaker known as the Godfather, and Pioneer, of LinkedIn Video and one of the world's premiere live-streaming & video marketing experts who's insights have been featured on NASDAQ, ROKU and a #1 Best-selling live-streaming book. As Founder & CEO of Voice Your Vibe, Brian has 20+ years of proven Digital Marketing experience strategizing with Fortune 500 brands across the globe and has been recognized as a 'LinkedIn Top Voice', 'LinkedIn Video Creator Of The Year', one of the 'Top 50 Most Impactful People of LinkedIn' and a 'LinkedIn Global Leader of The Year' for two consecutive years. Named "2020 Best LIVE Festive Show of The Year" at the IBM TV Awards, his two weekly LIVE shows have been featured in Forbes, Thrive Global, Yahoo Finance, an Amazon best-selling book and syndicated on a Smart TV Network.

55. Chris Curran

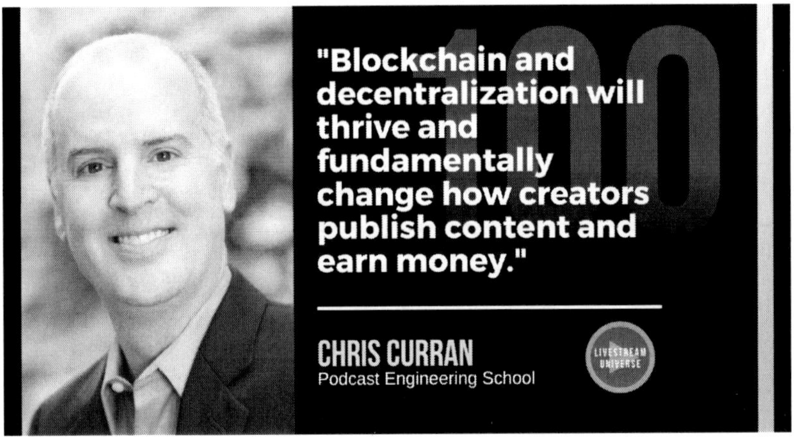

Blockchain and decentralization will thrive and fundamentally change how creators publish content and earn money, as well as how audience members consume content and support their favorite creators.

Chris Curran is an Audio engineer, podcast producer, host of The Podcast Engineering Show, music producer, musician, songwriter, author of Leap Beyond Your Limits. He is the founder & lead instructor at the Podcast Engineering School.

56. AI ADDYSON-ZHANG

2022 will be the year of video, especially monetization through video content in the e-commerce space. Amazon Live offers content creators a great opportunity to create content and monetize it. Other livestreaming platforms such as Facebook, LinkedIn, and Instagram will probably catch up in 2022.

Dr. Ai Addyson-Zhang is a professor turned entrepreneur. She is the founder of Classroom Without Walls and an Adobe Education Leader, Adobe Insider, and HubSpot Academy Instructor. Her work has been featured in Forbes, Pearson Education, Today Show, and more.

57. Christoph Trappe

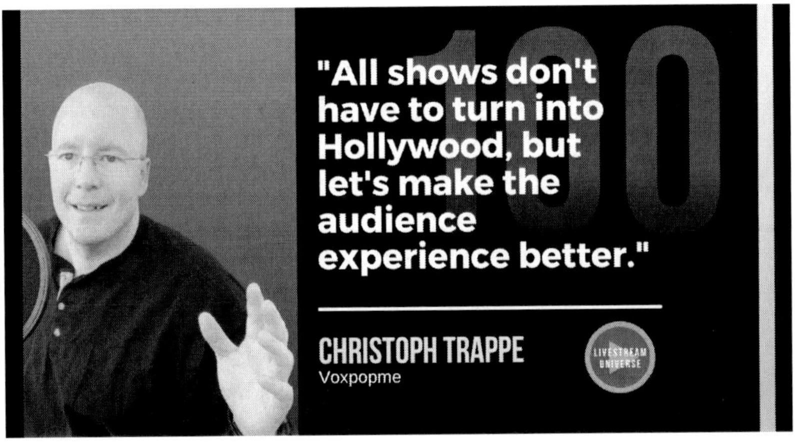

With more brands doing podcasts and now livestreams, the time has come for production value to go up. Yes, not everything is perfect, but bad audio, lighting or other "easy-to-fix" tech issues will become more of an issue. That doesn't mean all shows have to turn into Hollywood, but let's make the audience experience better.

Christoph Trappe creates experiences useful to people interested in understanding their customers. He's a Top 100 CX thought leader, Top 5% Global Podcaster, Content Strategist and author of "Going Live."

58. John Pretto

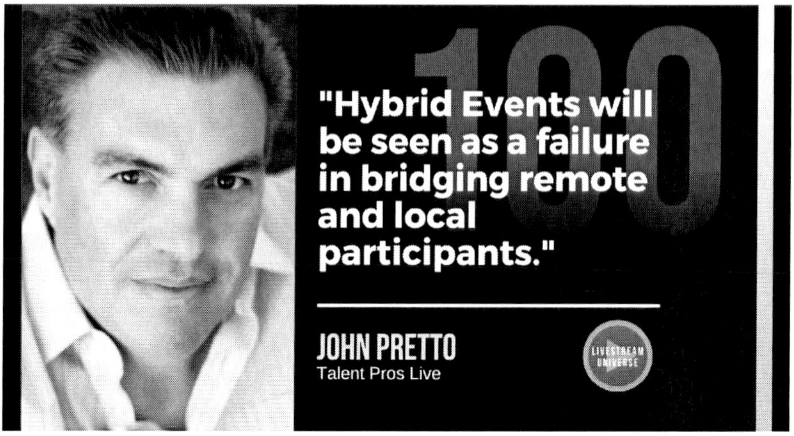

1. Microsoft teams will continue to improve their SDKs, API's and will lead Zoom programmability versus Zoom.

2. Hopin's Market Valuation will fall by 25%

3. Hybrid Events will be seen as a failure in bridging remote and local participants

John Pretto is a 25 year veteran in Streaming and Digital Media.

59. Jaime Cohen

Social audio has had a slow burn for years but took off in 2020 and 2021 . In 2022 it will be next level. With remote work continuing for the foreseeable future we'll see companies developing voice-only internal social media. Platforms like Clubhouse may create a paid business version of their platform to get the jump on that market.

Jaime Cohen, founder of The Right Words, is an internationally recognized speaker, communication coach & advisor, LinkedIn Learning author, and top LinkedIn creator whose communication-focused content has amassed millions of views. She transforms high achievers into powerhouse communicators who get the job, land that promotion, build thought leadership online, and become stronger leaders.

60. Eddie Garrison

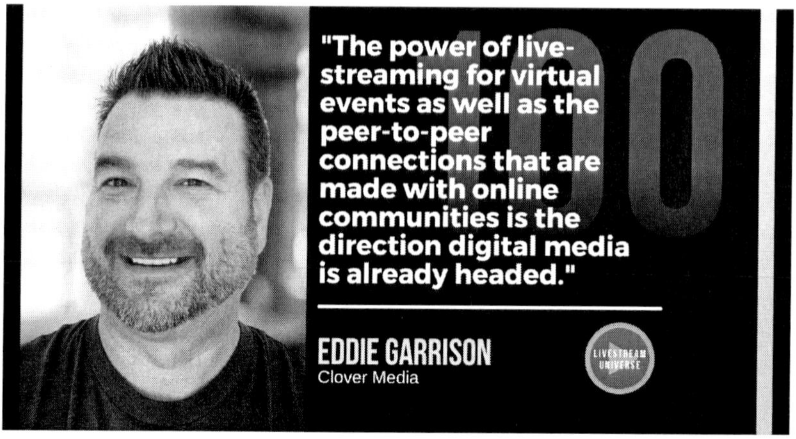

We will really begin to see the power of online communities even more so than we did in 2021. The power of livestreaming for virtual events as well as the peer-to-peer connections that are made with online communities is the direction digital media is already headed. Not unlike real-life communities, online communities look to serve a specific target audience to help one another better themselves. To teach, to learn and to connect.

Eddie Garrison helps brands grow their Digital Presence by utilizing the power of Social Media with real World Strategy, Design & Results!

61. Zef Zan

Post pandemic, a LIVE video is the new norm of meeting, connecting and engaging with one another online (even though it is NOT a new technology!). During the pandemic, it certainly has become an essential tool in the events space. Why? Because a LIVE video is the next best thing to being in the same room with the other person! As event tech continues to grow rapidly in 2022 (and it #Zefinitely will), not leveraging LIVE videos in your event design can mean that you're leaving money on the table! Virtual or hybrid event creators, producers and other event professionals need to explore ways to integrate LIVE videos into their event design to help drive attendee, sponsor and exhibitor participation, to create memorable event experiences and/or to maximize event ROI. Boom!

Zef Zan is a LIVE Broadcast & Virtual Events Producer at Vendor Shows LIVE & We Do Virtual Events LIVE. She's all about helping you create, produce and host DYNAMIC + ENGAGING virtual event experiences that get to YE$ connections.

Her 200mph energy is her superpower AND she uses it to help you SHOW UP + SHINE your light a little brighter!

62. H. Dean Reynolds

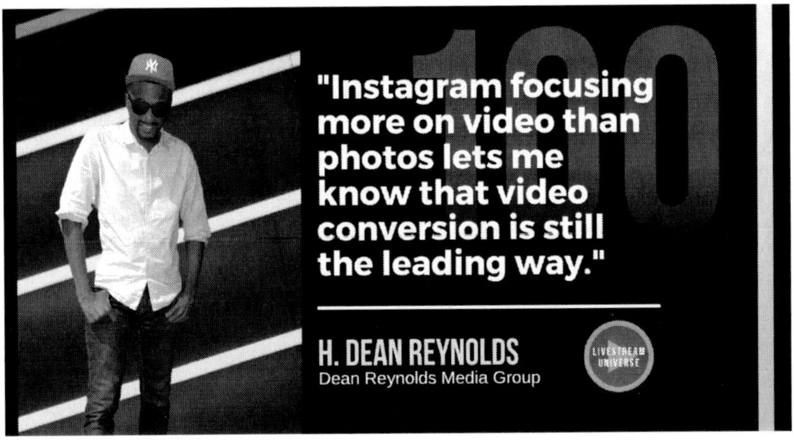

As a content creator, the fact that Instagram is now focusing more on video than photos lets me know that video conversion is still the leading way consumers prefer! Can you imagine YouTube now has its TikTok version?! Yass! YouTube Shorts! but wait, Facebook also has "Facebook Reels" OMG.

H. Dean Reynolds is a licensed music publisher who is certified by YouTube Music. He also has a strong video and TV background and serves as the creative director for Dean Reynolds Media Group

63. Tim Gillette

In 2022 I see more people creating Video Podcasts using storytelling. In years past many large media created short shows, now many independents will create shows.

Tim Gillette is the Creator of Simple Easy Marketing and Branding. Hosting Live and Virtual events around online marketing using blogs, video blogs, and podcasts to build a business, Tim started in the speaking business after a personal conversation with a friend and mentor Zig Ziglar, who inspired Tim to find a way to be himself and his message with the world just by being himself.

64. Claudia Santiago

We are in a major revolution! Being in the entertainment industry, I see this as akin to eras in history when there were major shifts: just as when the cassette tape overtook records, then CDs overtook the cassette tape and digital replaced analog recordings and midi instruments took over! The amazing thing is today we are able to do much more than we could do years ago.

We have also seen COVID, a global pandemic, force many to change the way they do life and business. The entertainment and hospitality/tourism industries will never be the same and are having to pivot quickly and frequently. I see this as an opportunity to welcome the new and allow activation of the creative innovation power within each of us at a whole new level! We live in exciting times… that is if we don't stay stuck in the old.

I see that moving forwards in 2022, we will find new platforms opening up, current platforms changing their focus and systems.

New, new, new! is the name of the game. I sense that there will be a resurgence of new work opportunities for coaching as new systems and strategies will overwhelm the online space in various ways such as NFT. There will be a period of time in which embracing and incorporating these new strategies, software and systems will be key for brands and companies to gain market share and sustainability in this new world of business. Education, community and a willingness to grow and embrace the new will be the key to success.

Regardless of the pandemic and incredible tech changes, remaining connected in relationships within authentic communities will be another key to success and health to balance such huge transitions as we are relational beings, not robots, and this is a foundation not to toss aside. I see health and wellness developing new strategies to help mentor people as they transition to the new.

Claudia Santiago is an international recording artist, live entertainer and seasoned professional performer at local, national and international private and corporate live events with extensive touring, tv, radio and media appearances. Claudia's expertise also extends as a strong online entertainer, brand influencer, speaking talent and consultant.

65. JEFFREY BRADBURY

In 2022, microblogging, and microstreaming will continue to take off. The ability to quickly create short amounts of content will further dominate the marketplace and help us fill the needs of our dopamine-driven fantasies.

Jeff Bradbury is the creator of the TeacherCast Educational Network at TeacherCast.net.

66. John R. DiStefano, Jr.

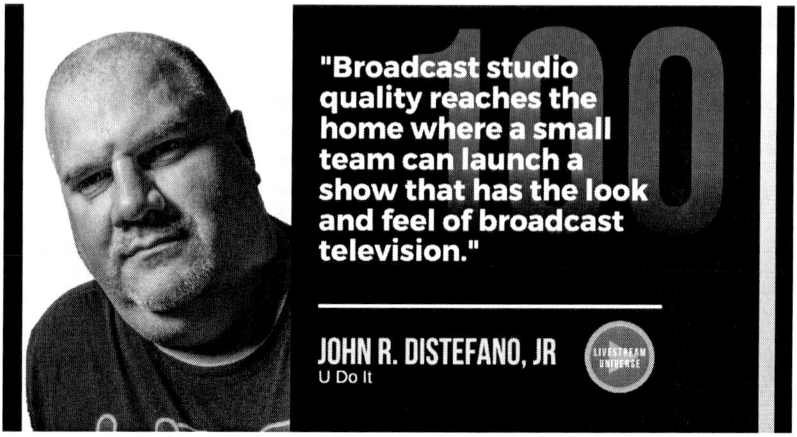

Now that livestreaming is mainstream the companies are receiving a wealth of feedback. I believe 2022 is the year that the livestreaming broadcast companies will respond to these requests and it will be glorious! We're already seeing integration with Stream Deck, co-host collaboration with studio control and the ability to stream to 30+ platforms simultaneously.

I think 2022 is the year that broadcast studio quality reaches the home where a small team of co-hosts or host and producer combinations can launch a show that has the look and feel of broadcast television. Scene switching, soundFx triggers, lighting automation, camera zoom/pan, screensharing, guest swapping and more will all be features that a co-host or producer will be able to control remotely while allowing the host to run the show without distraction.

John R. DiStefano, Jr. produced DIY content on YouTube that has now morphed into a side hustle working with Derral Eves and others developing software solutions to implement their vision. He is also CEO of No Cheese Records, which is a record label focusing primarily on hip-hop and EDM.

67. Bee Smith

My prediction is that in 2022, you will see a double portion of new livestream apps that come with added features of previous ones to better help users reach target audiences.

Bee Smith is a Global 4-time bestselling author and award-winning Mental Health Advocate. Overcoming Suicide she uses her multimedia gifts to shine the light on Mental Health issues and encourages others to walk without shame and live a life full of Joy!

68. Phil Kluba

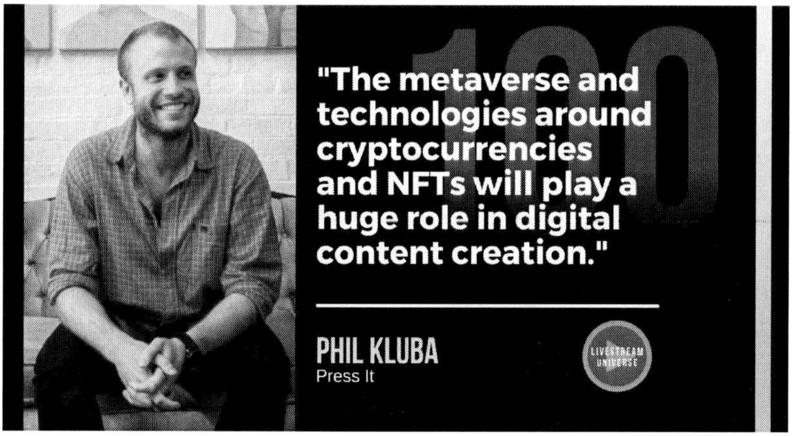

I believe the metaverse and the technologies around cryptocurrencies and NFTs will play a huge role in digital content creation. There will be new and immersive ways to create courses, sell products, tell stories, and build virtual events in 2022. The worlds of virtual, augmented, and traditional media will blend and build the foundation of internet 3.0. The technologies we use to create will improve and become more hands-on, making it easier for creators to create.

Phil Kluba is the founder & CEO of Press It, a Toronto-based media production company that has spent the past seven years specializing in innovative video, live-streaming, and content solutions.

69. Carlos Phoenix

Livestreaming remains a fantastic way for individuals and businesses to reach their target audiences. As a dealer in the tools and tech to simplify and expand on livestreaming, the next step is expanding the reach by first improving the quality of streams from graphics to sophistication and expansion of the distribution of content... including television. Smart TV platforms can expand such reach to target audiences. I offer such capabilities and it will grow in 2022.

Carlos Phoenix currently offers great tools, both hardware and software, to help expand the capabilities of those creating live and recorded content at home, office and mobile. He is building a platform for content distribution on all media platforms including television.

70. Chip Edwards

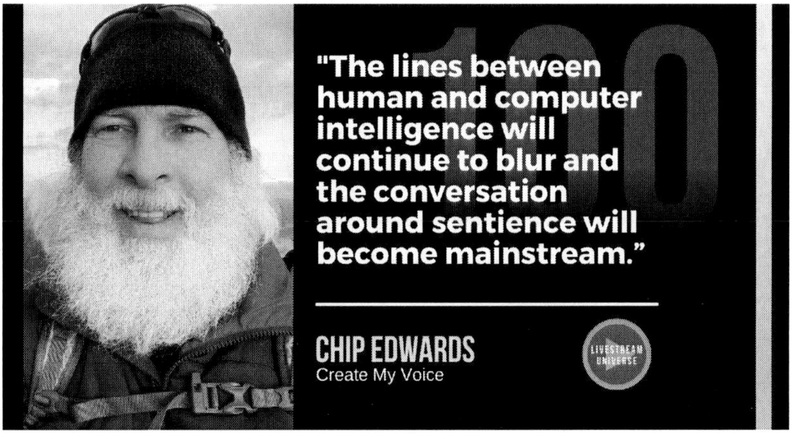

Artificial Intelligence (AI) will make significant inroads into media creation. Marketing material, news stories, blog posts, and course creation will all be significantly aided (or in some cases fully automated) by computers generating the copy. Well-written, unique, interesting stories will be entirely generated by Artificial Intelligence. The lines between human and computer intelligence will continue to blur and the conversation around sentience will become mainstream. Relying on Voice Assistants like Amazon Alexa and Google Assistant will continue to expand and more content producers will use this platform to engage their market. And as everyone gets used to talking to these devices (and getting personalized responses), the line between human and robot will blur further.

Chip Edwards of Create My Voice helps content producers (bloggers and podcasters) deliver their content through Voice Assistant platforms. Now anyone can just ask for your content (and hear it).

71. Toni Henderson-Mayers

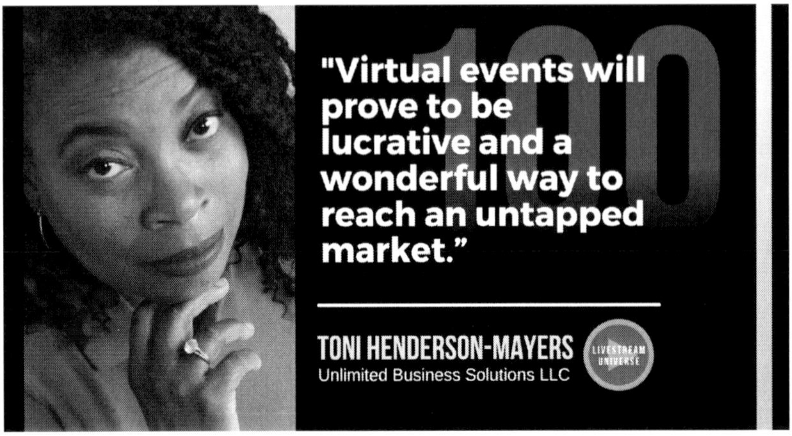

Virtual events are here to stay. This will not take away from in-person events; it will be an option. It will be an option that will prove to be lucrative and a wonderful way to reach an untapped market.

An entrepreneur for over 30 years, Toni Henderson-Mayer's success with branding and development of on and offline businesses such as Wise Courtship, Alphabet Theater Workshop, Word Therapy Publishing and UB Solutions has positioned her as a top business coach in the areas of organizational management, digital marketing, training and HR services for private and government clients.

72. Brian Wallace

As I have said in previous years, LinkedIn continues to be an underrated livestreaming asset. Viewers can watch a replay of your live video so the repurposing of it is great. Since last year, LinkedIn has created creator mode and now offers more people the opportunity to become live broadcasters. I am excited to see what the LinkedIn creator community comes up with next!

Brian Wallace is the Founder of NowSourcing, a top-rated content marketing agency that makes the world's ideas, simple, visual, and influential.

73. Marco Novo

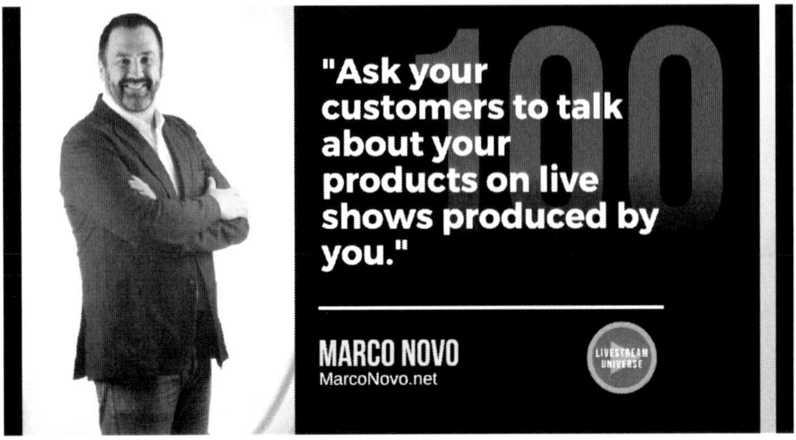

"People Like Me" approach livestreaming, influencer marketing and word of mouth as going together. First, let me give you a fast, non-academic overview of these three concepts as discussed in this context:

1. **Livestreaming:** Real time video with the possibility to interact with viewers and speakers.
2. **Influencer marketing:** When people with a sphere of influence (celebrity, thought leader, expert) recommend a certain product or service.
3. **Word of mouth:** When someone I know recommends a product or service to me based on their experience with that product/service, based on my needs.

Amazon is leading this approach by allowing everyday people to talk on live shows about their favorite products. You just need to have a following on a given social media platform, apply to become an Amazon influencer, and if you're approved, you can go live and talk about your favorite Amazon items. Sounds great, right? But there's a tiny problem, which can become big. You're on rented land, so Amazon can stop the program, and you're "out of the road", or you can be restricted by Amazon rules.

So, the best option is to have your own space. You can use tools to embed shows on your website and do your live shows there. Your house, your rules. And how can you apply the "People Like Me" approach? Asking your customers to talk about your products on live shows produced by you. What they love about them, how they use them, how they can be improved (yes, it is good to leave the honesty door open). Your customers will love to share their experiences, thoughts, and opinions about what you're selling, your viewers will get a truthful experience (they are "people like them") and it will not be an expensive approach, which will have an interesting ROI.

Everyday, more people are getting familiar with livestreaming, technology is more user-friendly, and Internet speed is increasing, which facilitates the process. In addition, think about making some exclusive events for your better customers, and think about bringing some on-screen. Make special offers, create scarcity just for the show, and so on. This approach uses the power of word of mouth as it's people like me recommending; Influencer marketing as they know what they are talking about; and livestreaming as I can interact with them in real-time. So, why not give it a try?

Marco Novo is a Portuguese live streamer, live remote producer, live stream consultant and trainer.

74. Marisa Cali

Audio is extra important when livestreaming. Bad audio will make you lose your audience no matter if you're talking for a few minutes or an hour-long session. With the rise of audio-focused events, virtual event organizers will consider adding an audio-only option for eventgoers. A downloadable option will be key to planning and offering one more connection point.

Connection points engage your audience more than just for the main event and continuously over time with repurposing. Audio-specific content made a huge splash with apps like Clubhouse and Twitter Spaces and their popularity proved that audiences ARE in fact consuming on-demand audio.

With the rise of livestreaming and increasing demand for video content, Marisa Cali found a calling in remote live stream production. In April 2020, she launched the Live on Social Now Productions division of her business which blends her love of tech, project management, and creativity.

Marisa has had the pleasure of working with exceptional partners to execute virtual summits, exclusive fireside chats, and podcasts that build community.

75. LELAND BEST

Three words – "Remote-Controlled Broadcasting." As our world continues to get smaller, thanks primarily to audio and video technology coming to the forefront during the pandemic of 2020, we can expect to see many more working their movie-making magic at keyboards and control stations from their personal home studios, rather than a remote stage facility.

"The Cloud" has been, and will continue to be the major threshold to be crossed in order to reach the pinnacle level of near-infinitely scalable broadcast production. Twitter is out, LI is still boring, YouTube will stumble once again, Twitch will see an uptick in content variety other than gamers, and live-streaming websites and other online a/v services will continue to lock, pop, and drop for years to come.

As one who's been involved since the inception of real-time, high-definition audio and video production over the internet, I can say this... we are still to this day, only ever in it for the personal, relationship-building experience this medium allows us to have in a moment's notice with anyone from practically anywhere around the globe! Allowing grassroots broadcasters like ourselves to circumnavigate the biased, and propagated media created in the mainstream.

Leland Best is the Owner/Operator of BestLIVE.tv, co-owner and Sr. Technical Director of Talent Pros LIVE, where the team just completed this year's annual "National Overdose Prevention Leadership Summit" for 2021 for the second year in a row. He's worked as a remote technical director for clients such as: IDOtv.com, the Public Health Institute, and the Professional Referee Organization for MLS.

76. Erin Cell

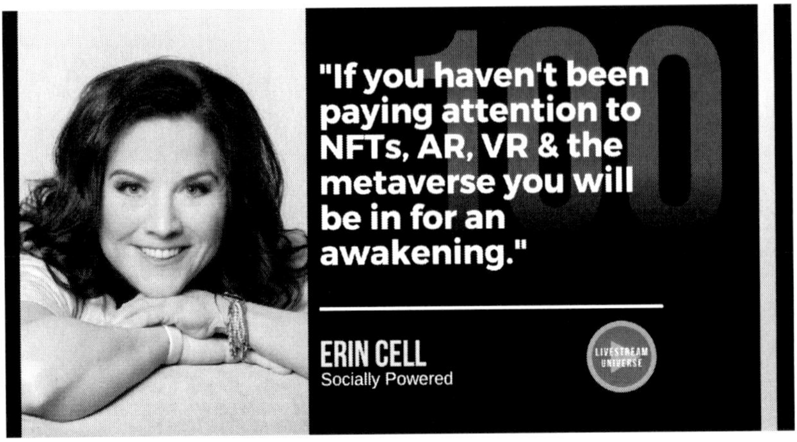

The announcement of Facebook entering the metaverse speaks volumes for what we can expect for the future of digital media and marketing. We are entering a new world & if you haven't been paying attention to NFTs, AR, VR and the metaverse you will be in for an awakening. I think you will start to see all of these media become more prevalent in the mainstream. This means it will open up a whole new world for marketing to people in other realities.

Erin Cell currently manages & produces the Bad Crypto Podcast and the Nifty Show Podcast. Both shows are focused on blockchain technology and the future of digital collectibles.

77. Phil Gerbyshak

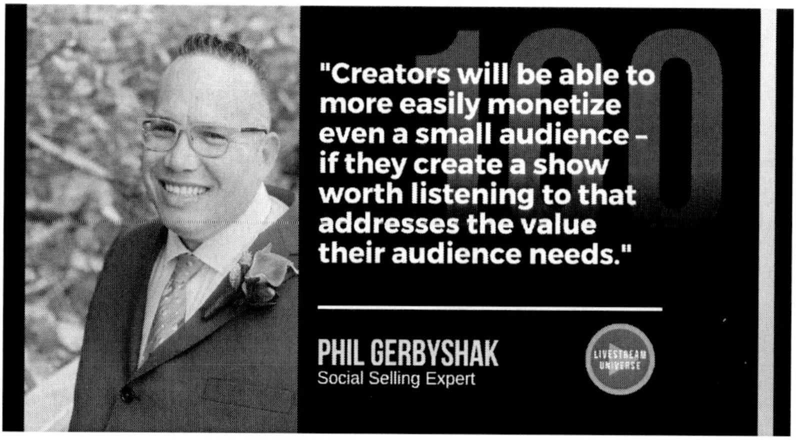

2022 will be the year social media and podcasting gets more intimate, with smaller communities of people being the goal and the outcome of a confluence of political angst, Facebook continuing to lose our trust, and content producers finally realizing the true power of the quality of their audience. With tools like Kajabi offering easy private RSS feeds, creators will be able to more easily monetize even a small audience – if they create a show worth listening to that addresses the value their audience needs.

Phil Gerbyshak is a social selling and sales expert, working with service-based professionals like financial advisors, insurance professionals and consultants to improve their productivity, performance and profitability. He hosts the Social Selling Essentials show, and a book by the same name will be out in Q1 of 2022.

78. Dan Hughley

The bar for sound quality has risen in podcasting as more and more shows emerge that just sound great. In the coming year, I expect to see more podcasters feeling empowered to record, edit, and mix their own content for publication rather than rely on the skills of an audio engineer. I also see the popularity of the one-stop-shop that does all of that for you, plus helps with booking guests, writes show notes, posts on socials etc., gaining popularity. This isn't because of the skills involved, but the time. And as software developers and equipment manufacturers continue making products that allow storytellers to create content without having to think much about technology, the product is going to be great-sounding content from every level of podcaster.

Dan Hughley is an audio engineer who wants to help podcasters simplify the recording process. His current role as Senior Marketing Manager at Focusrite gives him the opportunity to work with all types of content creators.

79. Valerie Morris

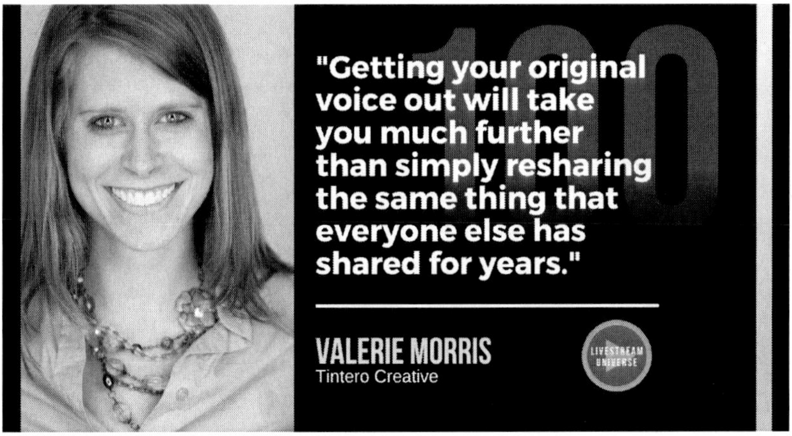

Ten years ago, brands could do really well by sharing/resharing third-party content that was relevant to their industry. However, today, there is SO MUCH content out there that viewers only want to spend their time on something that might have a new spin on the subject. That's why original content has become such a dominant force in marketing and social media. Whether you do that via podcasting, video, blogging, or something else, getting your original voice out is going to take you much further than simply resharing the same old thing that everyone else has shared for years.

Valerie Morris is a content marketing and social media expert. She and her team help clients create authority-building content to grow their brand awareness. Valerie is also a published author, public speaker and trainer, and active member in the digital marketing community. She also gives back through intern programs, industry organizations, and events to help students grow in their professions as well.

80. Gord Isman

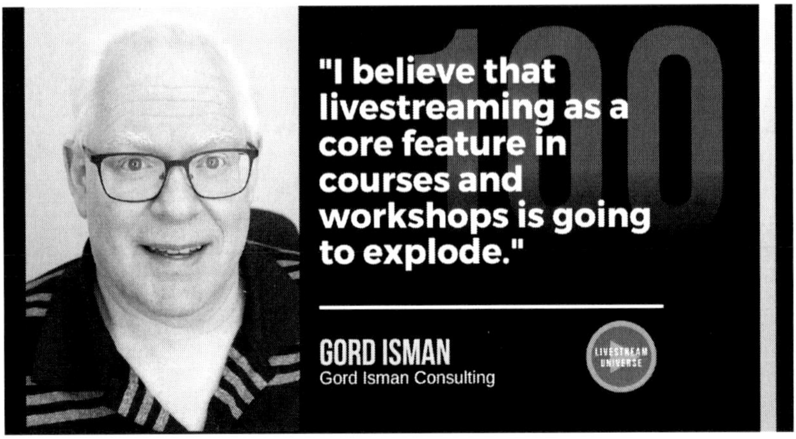

In our quickly changing world, LIVE taught transformational course/workshop experiences (e.g. cohort-based courses) via platforms like Zoom, enabling students to interact and engage with a coach/mentor/guide and supportive community at much deeper levels than pre-recorded, self-paced course content alone. As a result, people are more willing to step out of their comfort zones and take risks resulting in transformational outcomes in a shorter time.

I know that I've consumed my share of pre-recorded, self-paced courses that somehow didn't result in me moving my needle of progress forward. Maybe it's time to try a cohort-based course experience? I recently taught my own Cohort-Based Course on YouTube Channel Essentials and found that the students just loved the LIVE teaching, LIVE Q&As, and one-on-one Zoom coaching sessions that were all part of the package. I believe that livestreaming as a core feature in courses and workshops is going to explode!

Gord Isman is a Video and YouTube Consultant specializing in helping people to grow their businesses with video. He has a "How To" YouTube channel that educates people in video editing (e.g. Camtasia), video marketing and YouTube. Gord offers done-for-you services, courses, as well as one-on-one coaching to help you work through your video creation and content marketing challenges.

81. Brad Friedman

I predict 2022 will be the year Human-to-Human® #H2H marketing becomes more important than ever. As the Metaverse begins to take shape, consumers of content, who end up as consumers of goods and services, will consume from those brands they trust. And trust is built through Human-to-Human® marketing. Brands will be thinking more and more about whether their content is building trust and is segregated to the right audience. And, to do this, brands will realize the trust-building benefits of video, livestreaming and podcasts.

I believe most events will be hybrid events, giving brands fewer opportunities to engage with prospects in person. The psychological impact of COVID-19 will force brands to stop considering livestreaming their events as a bonus and start considering it a necessity. And I believe these livestreams will be more interactive. We'll see more polls, more influencers, and more short vertical video event-goers and others can watch on a mobile device. Quality trust-building content specifically targeted to the right audience will be essential in 2022. As will developing an interactive hybrid events strategy.

Brad Friedman, a Digital Marketing Strategist and Coach, is the Founder of The Friedman Group, LLC, a digital marketing agency that works with business owners and professional services providers to generate leads and revenue online. Brad is an Amazon best-selling author of two books and the host of The Digital Slice Podcast.

82. Christian Karasiewicz

Livestreaming will become more mainstream. We'll also see greater expansion into live shopping, with more brand sponsorships across all levels of streamers. Lastly, virtual try-ons of products and more will come more into focus.

Christian Karasiewicz is the Content Marketing Manager at StreamYard and host of the Launch Your Live show, where he shares streaming tips and gear recommendations. He is the host of Social Chatter, the longest-running social media marketing talk show from Social Chefs.

83. Marc Gawith

2022 is going to bring a change in the OTT, live and simulated live marketplace shifting the way we think about the "protocols" of livestreaming and video delivery. Solutions like RTMP will be an also-ran behind new more stable delivery methods like RSP, and others. Platforms that use RTMP will be forced to start developing for new, more current, protocols.

Mark Gawith is the Director of Business Development for Resi Media. He has been involved in live video streaming for 7 years having worked in consumer and enterprise livestreaming, from being a creator to now working with one of the top delivery platforms.

84. Chris Stone

As Influencer Marketing on live video continues to rise, I see not only the opportunities for Influencers to be massive – but especially to those that have their act together on live video. As Amazon has proven, the US is going to be the next major spot for online shopping – specifically live shopping with key influencers leading the way. I suspect that other major retailers such as Target, Costco and Wal-Mart and others begin to follow Amazon's trail and build out their platforms to allow for Influencers to help guide their consumer shopping behavior, right while they are live online.

It's especially exciting to those that have already curated a great livestream presence and following – because we've seen many approved Amazon influencers arrive on the platform without any livestreaming experience, coming from platforms where livestreaming isn't prevalent or used at all. Those Influencers who are able to drive consumer behavior on live video will have a distinct advantage as these additional platforms start to flip the "livestream shopping switch."

With a 25+ year history in the music industry with Sony, driven and passionate entrepreneur Chris Stone founded the Podcast and Livestreaming Consultancy Cast Ahead after the success of his own co-hosted podcasts changed his life. At Cast Ahead, Chris thrives on enabling driven entrepreneurs, influencers, thought leaders and enterprises to express their stories and elevate their reach while extending their efficiency in that process.

85. Rob Balasabas

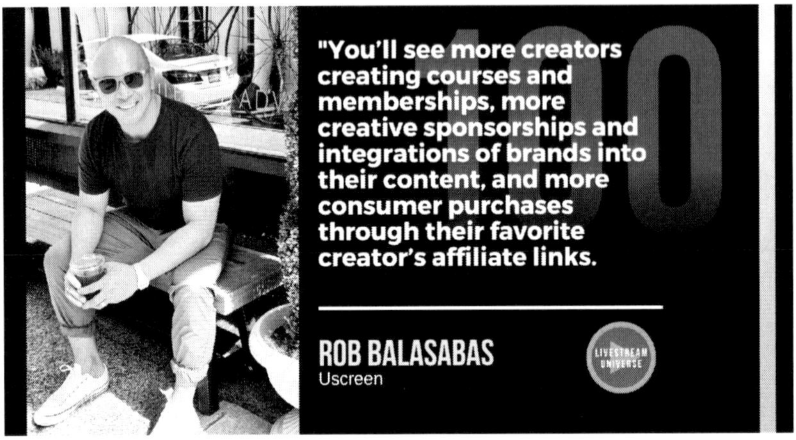

Content Creators will be diversifying their revenue streams much more in 2022. You'll see more creators creating courses and memberships, more creative sponsorships and integrations of brands into their content, and more consumer purchases through their favorite creator's affiliate links.

Rob Balasabas is a Content Creator on YouTube, sharing helpful advice and strategies with creators to build community, content, and revenue streams. He is the head of partnerships at Uscreen.

86. Eliseo Way

With live content becoming more and more normalized and dare I say preferred, we will start to see a shift from pre-recorded and programmed broadcast to real-time live on-demand content. We are already seeing brands like Amazon put livestreaming creators on the forefront of their platform and with their recent acquisition of MGM Studios, I expect to see Amazon using all of their new media outlets and channels to feature even more livesteaming creators. As this model becomes more popular, we will see companies like Netflix, Hulu, Disney Plus etc. etc. follow that formula by also opening up livestreaming channels for vetted creators. YouTube has already proven that even though people can easily find the pre-recorded content they are searching for to get the answers they need, most people will still chose to watch a livestream on that very same topic because it adds a new element to the experience that many people love, that being real-time Q&A sessions and exciting community engagement.

Eliseo Way is the Owner and operator of ContentEcosystem. He works with businesses, brands and individual influencers to help them create top-notch content.

87. Jim Fuhs

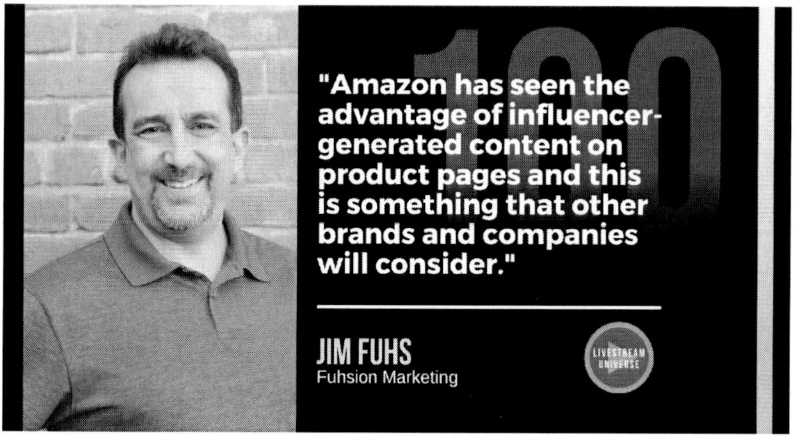

Shoppable Videos will continue to grow on platforms. Amazon has seen the advantage of influencer-generated content on product pages and this will become something that other brands and companies will consider. This allows user-generated content to go to a whole new level. Pinterest is starting to do this and I believe other platforms will follow suit and allow for affiliate revenue.

Jim Fuhs is an Amazon Influencer and cohost of the Amazon Live Show Dealcasters. He also does remote production work for companies like StreamYard, IBM Research, and the United Nations.

88. Brandon Birkmeyer

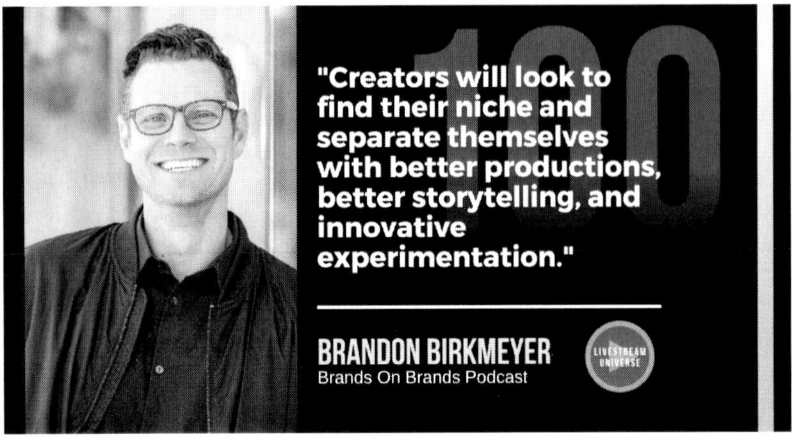

The Year of Creative Voices. We'll continue to see more people than ever tapping into new creative outlets. As we have new voices entering media at a faster pace, it will force more creativity into the space. To stand out from the growing crowd, creators will look to find their niche and separate themselves with better productions, better storytelling, and innovative experimentation.

Brandon Birkmeyer is a marketing coach who helps industry experts, coaches, and content creators build their brand. For over 17 years, Brandon directed brand strategy for top FORTUNE 100 companies. He now produces and hosts a top marketing podcast called Brands On Brands, which has ranked #1 in personal branding and content marketing.

89. Lottie Hearn

Having #MS issues off-camera – 2021 was a year watching big biz react to lockdown 2 using only vapid-virtual Zoom/Teams… Most ignoring the wider impact implications of quality LIVE tools. Some did basic talks at camera, others tracked employee hours. Many couldn't sit with screen stress + little interaction opportunities… Virtual-fatigue was THE 2021 real-life-pain #GlobaLIVE issue. So THANKS to our inclusive LIVE community! My 2022 prediction is that biz must now look beyond basic Zooming Teams, demand more "LIVE production" quality, using simple, self or LIVE producer controlled, virtual meeting rooms, with inspiring interactivity included. 2022 is time to own accessed anywhere, secure, one-click Video Chat rooms (eg. Whereby.com) – no log-in, stop on-screen overload & start paying proper attention to the impact of easy viewer interaction, not just speaker "lectures"… 2022 #LIVEPresenters will fully realize the importance of using Broadcast Quality #GlobaLIVE Tools & simple #LIVEStylePresenting – like Ross & everyone here helps the world with daily – thanks Ross!

#LIVEWithLottie Hearn – #ConfidenceOnCamera worldwide pro-speaker, mentor, coach – stage to screen for over 30 years. She even wrote the first book about it. Her latest health issues may take her out of LIVE, for now, but never stops her #GlobaLIVE support life!

90. Jesse Guthrie

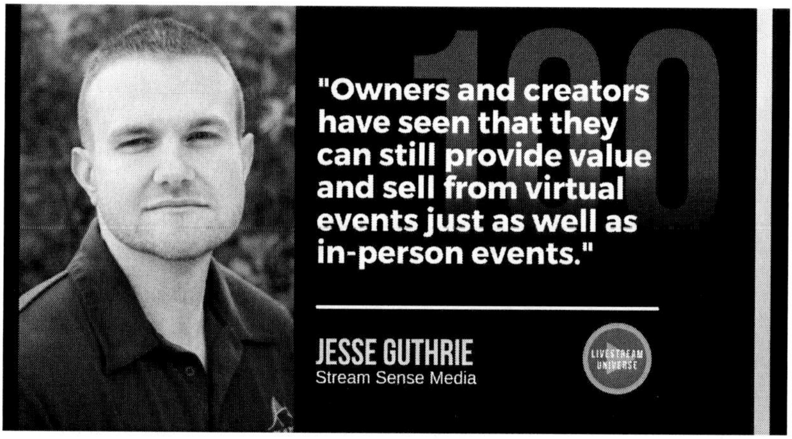

I think virtual events are here to stay based on the outcome of Covid-19. The owners and creators have seen that they can still provide value and sell from virtual events just as well as in-person events. The virtual event landscape is now forever changed. The use of production and level of graphics is now more important than ever!

Jesse Guthrie is the owner and head graphic master of Stream Sense Media. He has worked with companies such as Bass Pro Shops as well as Streamyard in his role of livestreaming and graphics jedi.

91. Tony Mobley

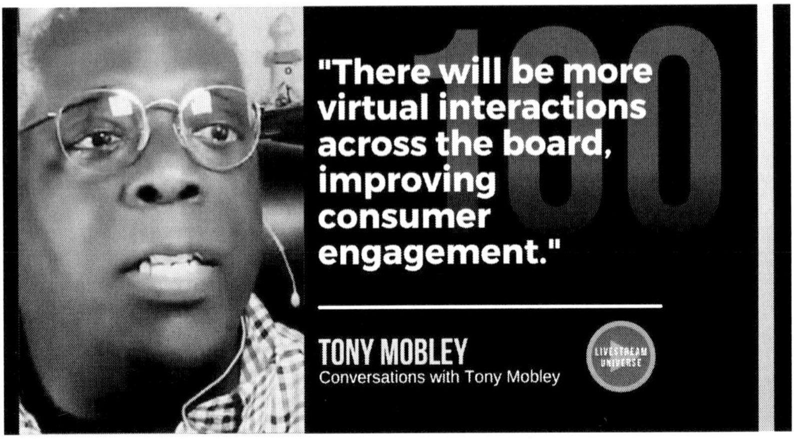

There will be more virtual interactions across the board in all areas you can think of! They will improve consumer engagement!

Tony Mobley is the creator of Conversations with Tony Mobley, real conversations with real people.

92. ASH BORLAND

We will see a move to a new content strategy that would include short vertical content (TikTok, REELS and Shorts) as this will be the brand discoverability but it will be paired with long-form livestreaming style content to build community. This approach will become the norm by the end of 2022.

Ash Borland is a Content Marketing Consultant & Top 20 UK Marketing Podcaster.

93. Wágner dos Santos

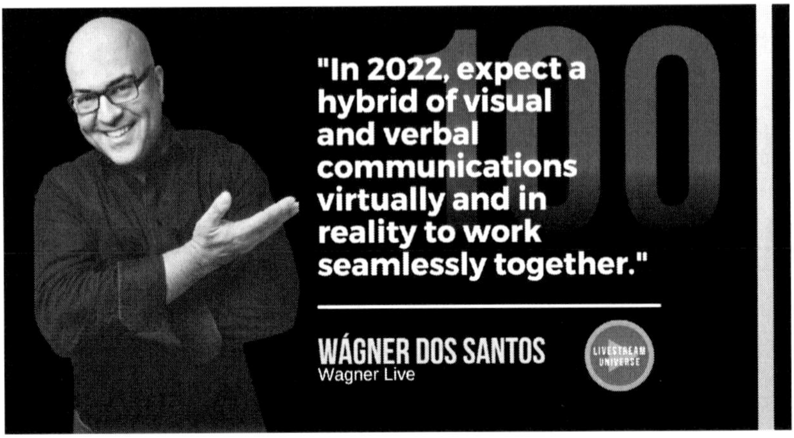

Despite several unfair remarks recently made by the media with respect to Facebook and Mark Zuckerberg, their considerable investment in the metaverse should not be ignored. While virtual worlds and experiences that liken "Ready Player One" may seem too fictional to believe today, there is no question that social networking/media is evolving more experientially. Human beings communicate best when their voices, likenesses, and body language are included because, arguably speaking, we are very complex and emotional creatures. Communicating in written form was a great introduction to the online world but it's very limiting. In 2022, expect a hybrid of visual and verbal communications virtually and in reality to work seamlessly together.

For over 5 years, Wágner dos Santos has been the creator and host of Wagner Live, a weekly podcast produced by The Wagner Agency. In each episode and together with a special guest, expect to hear fresh perspectives on what's hot in business right now.

For the past 20+ years he has enjoyed a fulfilling career in the advertising industry and is currently the President / Account Planner at The Wagner Agency.

94. SUE-ANN BUBACZ

The depth and speed of change in digital media and LIVE-streaming are stronger than ever, but it's an especially inspiring and fun time for digital creators as the playing field becomes increasingly accessible. But, while fewer barriers to the digital game make the use of digital media increasingly easier, affordable, and viable for all brands and businesses, doing it well isn't nearly as simple. Still, I love the power of digital for the little guy! Personal brands and small businesses can play in the big leagues, going head-to-head with big corporations and international brands. Standing out means having the ability to resonate with prospects, customers, and other stakeholders, directly. It means you are able to connect with the right people in the right way. But, a lot more goes into making these critical impressions and really engaging with an audience.

Of course, there are several value-added content pieces to master, software and marketing stack considerations, and things like strategic thinking, marketing plans, business goals, and objectives, etc., to examine. What's the right balance between analytics and creativity? How can you produce the best user experience via both content and design? What's the most effective way to turn your digital efforts into conversions, i.e., paying customers? There's a LOT TO IT!

Do You Connect Human-to-Human via Digital Channels?

But, in my view, the bottom line for digital success (as always) comes back to the human factor. H2H, or human-to-human, is what creates, maintains, and sustains businesses. The relationships you create through your digital and LIVE messaging are what matters most to grow your business. The value and originality you deliver with digital media to serve your customers make all the difference in how well you connect. Taking strategies, campaigns, and tactics further by executing your plans effectively, efficiently, and consistently is essential. Today's marketing is a conversation, and the digital platforms you engage in facilitate this concept to actively improve your results. Connecting with people productively and engagingly is the future of digital and LIVE work together. A human-first approach is the core digital strategy for success. Now. Before. And in the future.

As a business content creator, writer, and editor, Sue-Ann Bubacz crafts and produces high-quality, unique web content assets to help businesses connect with people and grow. Her tenacity, business experience, and creativity help clients from a fresh and strategic perspective to create digital impressions for an impressive digital footprint. Catch her at: WriteMixforBusiness.com or MSSYBiz.com.

95. Dr. Aikyna Finch

In 2022 there will be video in emails, texts and purchases. People will be using more videos in their Facebook and IG stores. They will spend more time on their phones and iPads creating the content live as they sell and develop.

Dr. Aikyna Finch of Technically Intuitive is a social media speaker, trainer and conference host! She features women in tech and people of color in social media so they have the platform where they truly shine and are seen for their value in the industry!

96. TIM SOHN

More brands will multistream. I always recommend to livestream to at least two destinations – at least one of them not being owned by Facebook, since the platform has become increasingly unreliable. By multistreaming, with a tool like StreamYard, you reach a bigger audience and reduce the chances of catastrophe if one of the social medias you are streaming to is down.

Tim Sohn is a 15-year leukemia survivor and founder of Sohn Social Media Solutions, where he produces & hosts livestreams for brands, nonprofits and entrepreneurs that want to create bigger impact, build relationships & community. He is also the co-host of The Tim & Jim Show and Showing Up: Perspectives On Cancer with Kara Oelker.

97. WILL SLAISE JR.

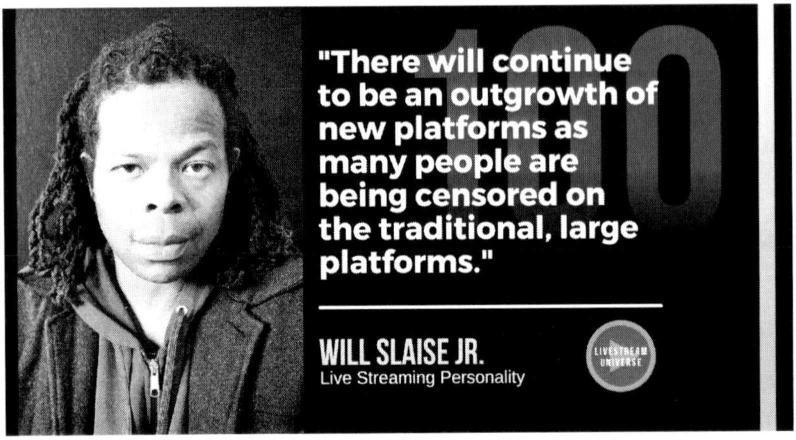

My predictions for livestreaming in 2022. The first one is, the larger platforms, such as Facebook and YouTube, will call for them to be regulated by the government. Why? To avoid any type of liability that could occur from content creators as well as any agendas or narratives that are perpetuated on that platform. The second prediction i have for 2022 is, there will continue to be, an outgrowth of new platforms. The reason for this is many people are being censored on the traditional, large platforms. They too, will have the desire, to have a place, where they can share their content and create their content.

The third and final prediction I have for 2022 is, the technology that is available, such as livestreaming platforms, cameras, encoders, software encoders, hardware encoders allows the average person to create content, share their content that helps others and in turn, makes the world a better place. This will continue to grow, at an exponential rate, even bigger than what it has in the past. One thing that this lockdown has shown us is, people still want to stay connected and people are still consuming great content. One of the best ways to create great content, as well as cut down your editing time, is to do livestreams.

Will Slaise Jr. produces digital content, as well as my podcast to teach,inspire and motivate others in the area of content creation (video, audio, digital files) and photography.

98. Junaid Ahmed

YouTube will continue to dominate in 2022. The company has transformed, taking in feedback from the creators and catering to just a massive audience with well thought out content and realism.

Through Home Studio Mastery, Junaid Ahmed has been helping content creators, podcasters, and speakers create their home studios, giving them an unparalleled advantage when they show up on video. A Dedicated home studio space also creates a deeper connection with peers and audience. Junaid has Designed studios for some of the top leaders on LinkedIn and Facebook.

99. Steffen Kaplan

Livestreaming Will Continue to Grow in Powerful, Helpful Ways. So much has changed in our world since the pandemic hit, including how we share information on social media. Although the spread of disinformation on social channels has contributed to what is now being termed an infodemic, social media is also used in many positive ways for social good — educating, raising awareness, raising funds, creating community and opportunity to help with many issues and problems in society.

Livestreaming has quickly become an essential way for brands and organizations of all types and sizes to communicate, share their mission, and grow globally. Even those who had never live streamed before quickly learned how to use the technology as they were home more than ever, due to COVID-19 upending life as we knew it. Livestreaming has become an invaluable component of social media, and its ability to reach so many viewers across multiple social channels simultaneously has captured the attention of millions of users and viewers.

But it is the personal connection that livestreaming creates, through sharing of insight, experiences, and stories, and most importantly, engaging with people in real-time — there is no hiding behind the screen, you are in full transparency mode as I say — that has attracted so many to live online broadcasts. Those that harness the power of creating great communities through the power of social media and livestreaming, will continue to grow in powerful and helpful ways!

Steffen Kaplan is a social media and visual strategist and live stream producer that has worked with AARP, The Pulitzer Prizes, and is the co-creator of the Martin Lindstrom and Marshall Goldsmith M&M Show live stream.

100. Lee Uehara

REPURPOSING CONTENT: My prediction is that more and more folks will find creative ways to repurpose their content, including recording more "rooms" on Clubhouse and turning them into podcast episodes. This will cause more people to buy upgraded equipment to get the job done.

GEAR/TECH: The trend to move to mirrorless cameras will continue to grow as they are lighter and faster, and in many cases smaller than DSLRs. In turn, there will be a great uptick in more video creation — and selfie headshots. Just remember, the best gear is the gear you can afford.

Lee Uehara, host of House of Lee NYC, is the co-founder of AAP (Asian American Podcasters Association), Podthon.com, the indie collective, and NYC Podcasters Network. Lee is also a rockstar photographer to podcasters and speakers.

PART III
IDEAS AND STRATEGIES

1. Justin Brown

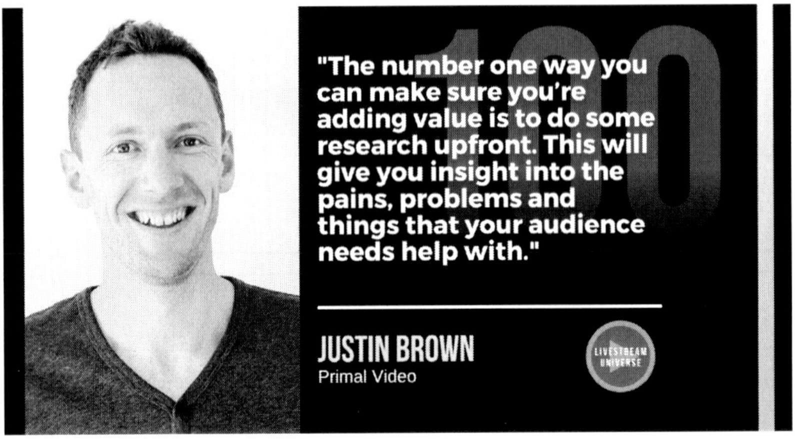

If you're a content creator in 2022, the most important thing you can do is focus on adding value for your followers or viewers. It doesn't matter what platform you're on and it doesn't matter whether you're livestreaming, podcasting or email marketing. If you aren't providing value - your followers will find another creator who is.

The number one way you can make sure you're adding value is to do some research upfront. This will give you insight into the pains, problems and things that your audience needs help with. You're then able to strategically create content that you know there's demand for and that people actually want. This optimized content is more likely to add value and succeed.

Justin Brown is a Netflix-featured producer and video marketing specialist helping entrepreneurs leverage the power of online video. After 20+ years in professional video, Justin created the Primal Video YouTube channel (1M+ subscribers), growing it to a 7-figure annual business.

2. Kate Skavish

Tip #1: Focus more on the quality of the content, not quantity. In 2022 all social platforms will follow the data and continue to favor live videos over other content forms. This, along with the trend to remote work, will bring more brands, industries, and individuals to livestreaming. As consumers experience content saturation, the competition for viewers' eyeballs will grow. Naturally, watchers' attention will be directed at more focused, better prepared, well thought through, pro-looking, and more entertaining personalities, shows, and brands.

Livestreaming combined with reels, stories and any other short-form videos will provide great opportunities to build and expand the reach of brands and businesses, including personal brands. The success will favor those who leverage the networking and create new opportunities for co-marketing, cross-selling, and other forms of partnerships.

Tip #2: If you don't live stream on Amazon Live yet, consider applying right now. I believe that Amazon will take the central stage in expanding and evolving the video marketing industry this year. In 2021 Amazon created a perfect environment where influencers and consumers collide at the right place at the right time. Never before was it as easy for the influencers to educate, guide, and help shoppers make the right decisions at the perfect moment.

Live videos will create a boom, if not a revolution, in online shopping. The consumer's demand is high and the competition is low. The window of opportunities will be wide open for those who plan to use livestreaming for e-commerce. We will see more personal brands and influencers on Amazon shopping.

Kate Skavish - a serial Entrepreneur, Co-founder of Wave.video - an online video editing, livestreaming, and hosting platform for marketers. Kate has over a decade of experience in video marketing and has built a successful multimillion-dollar business. Her mission is to make complex technology easy and accessible for everyone.

3. Aaron Linne

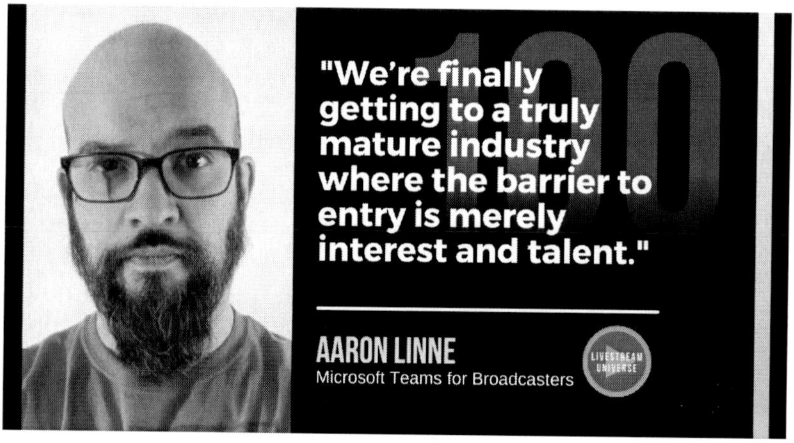

My son doesn't watch cartoons.

When I was growing up, the weekdays were for watching the Teenage Mutant Ninja Turtles and the weekend was ripe with new content. Monday through Thursday was the Super Mario Bros Super-Show, with Friday being the Legend of Zelda. Watching a real person on TV was mostly just when my family wanted to watch something and the closest thing to reality TV was the news.

My son doesn't watch cartoons. He's in 3rd grade and he watches his favorite people play his favorite games on YouTube. He watches tutorials about how to make games, reviews so he knows how to critique his Transformer toys, and I know I need to save up some money because he's started watching videos on how the Imagineers make animatronics at Disney.

All of this content is being produced in home studios, through hardware from the likes of Blackmagic Design or maybe even just a

Logitech webcam paired with a Blue Yeti. I know because I watch videos from guys like EposVox and Alex Lindsay who do reviews of all the tech I want so I know how to critique it... just like Transformer toys.

The technical delta between amateur and professional is being eradicated as more and more technology is democratized to being more accessible to everyone. The industry is changing where the knowledge of how much data an SDI cable can throughout is irrelevant; instead, we're finally getting to a truly mature industry where the barrier to entry is merely interest and talent.

There is a YouTube channel called "Primitive Technology" with over 10 million subscribers. It's a video series watching people build crazy complex structures out of mud and whatever they find in nature out in the bush of Australia. It's fascinating because of the skill of what is being built from just the natural resources around them. The technology fades into the background until you begin to pick It all apart. You're sitting on your couch on your big screen television watching guys build huts in 4K and you are mesmerized.

The future of streaming is straightforward: talent. There are enough tutorials to learn just about anything. Equipment can be purchased at discounts to improve your production values. There is enough going on in the world that you can pick out just about any topic and begin to create content.

Talent is where the future lies. Strengthening and refining your talent is the path to success. Being introspective to find what you are not good at and choosing to build that or simply not bother with that is the path forward to prune or build yourself into what you're wanting your life and career to be.

You have to just do it. Find the right cadence that works for you, whether it's once a month or once a week or once a day, find what you're trying to build and build it. As a product manager I started out making sure I spoke to a direct customer once a week; now it's almost a different customer every day directly talking about the future of media production through Microsoft Teams on Microsoft Teams. Make a video. Email a hero. Plug in that cord that's been lying in the garage that you've just been waiting to set up.

The new accessibility to technology isn't just coming, it's already here. Products like Teams and Zoom bring guests and titans of the industry right into your production setup. Companies like Elgato and AJA make hardware to produce a show right on your desk. Just pick a direction and go forward.

If I could give only one tip to the future of production, it is that there is no reason to wait for the future to get here. We are creating the future by making content today, in the present. Make your content, make your production and make your own future.

Aaron Linne is the senior product manager at Microsoft Teams for Professional Broadcast Solutions. He previously served as Microsoft's senior product manager of Skype for Content Creators, building features and partnerships for YouTube, Twitch and Mixer.

4. Bryan Kramer

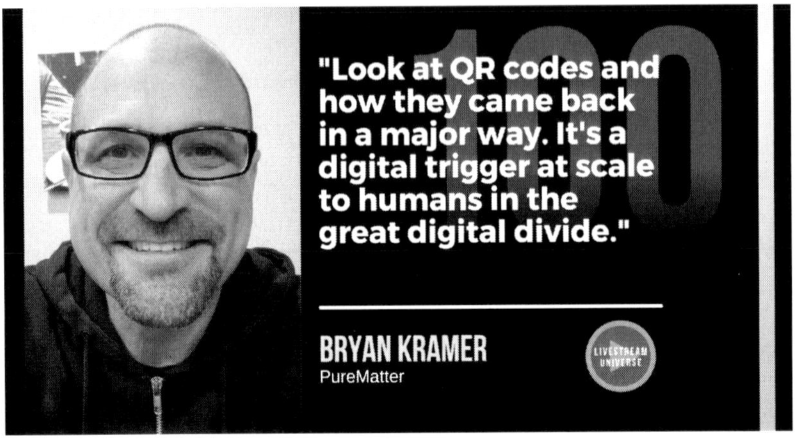

Connect online with offline in every instance. Look at QR codes and how they came back in a major way. It's a digital trigger at scale to humans in the great digital divide.

Bryan Kramer is the Proud Father of Human-to-Human: H2H. He's a Mentor and coach for entrepreneurs and leaders to accelerate their businesses in pre-burnout. He's the CEO at H2H Companies & PureMatter Agency, and a Keynote and TEDTalk speaker.

5. Katie Fawkes

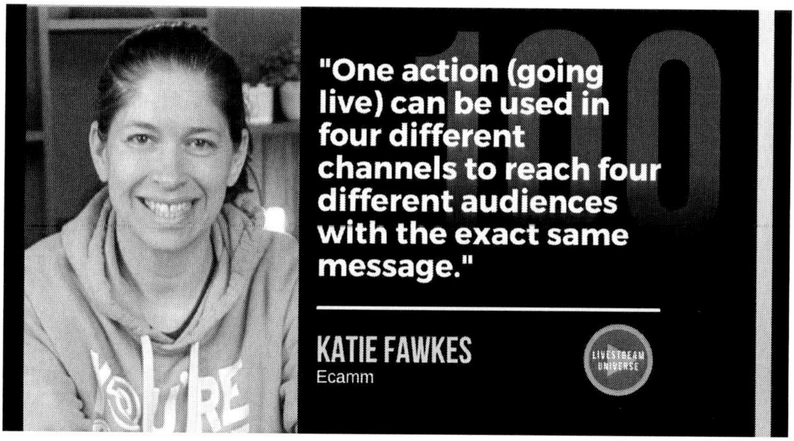

One of the most important things that content creators can do this year is to develop a strategic content plan. If you plan ahead, you'll only need to create the content once and can leverage it in different ways across multiple channels. For example, start with a well-planned live stream that delights your live viewers, trim down and optimize the video for replay viewers, grab the transcript to turn that content into a blog post, and pull out the audio to create a podcast. One action (going live) can be used in four different channels to reach four different audiences with the exact same message.

Katie Fawkes has been working in Content Marketing for fifteen years, starting her career in copywriting and growing into social media, video, and livestreaming. At Ecamm Network, Katie gets to work alongside some of the most amazing live streamers and content creators out there, helping them reach their goals and grow their business using video marketing and livestreaming.

6. Ian Anderson Gray

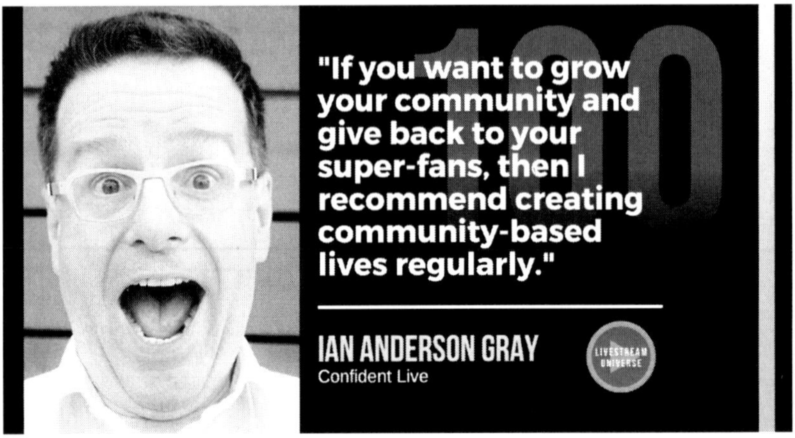

Creating a live video strategy is vital. Live video for live video's sake, or doing it because everyone else seems to be doing it, is not a smart reason. In 2022 I believe there are three types of live video most of us should be embracing, and a fourth type for some of us.

#1 Content Repurposing Machines

Creating quality content is hard work. And it's even harder now that our audiences are more fragmented. Once you've planned and set up a process, it's really easy to go live and turn it into a content repurposing machine. You can repurpose your live shows into podcasts, blog posts, short form video (for Instagram Reels and Tik Tok), and more. It's also the perfect antidote to perfectionism, since live video is never going to be perfect. When doing this, it's important to keep in mind your three audiences. Firstly, you have your live audience, then you have your replay audience who is watching in the future, and finally your podcast listeners who are listening in the future can't see what's going on.

#2 Community-based Lives

Creating content for repurposing is great, but creating engaging live content for your audience is vital. If you want to grow your community and give back to your super-fans, then I recommend creating Community-based lives regularly. These focus solely on the live element and aren't about repurposing at all. They can be raw and they don't need to be snazzy and professional. They're about you hanging out with your community, answering questions, and giving back to your audience.

#3 Group-based Live Training

Creating educational live training in groups is a great way to demonstrate your knowledge and value. Depending on your strategy, they can be offered for free (for community building) or paid.

#4 Live Shopping

This isn't for everyone, but for some of us, embracing live shopping is a smart move. Amazon Live has been around for a while, but Facebook, YouTube and Instagram Live are all getting into the live shopping world.

Ian is the founder of the Confident Live Marketing Academy and is the host of the Confident Live Marketing Podcast. He helps entrepreneurs to level up their impact, authority and profits by using live video confidently. Ian trained as a professional singer and lives near Manchester in the UK.

7. MELODY JOHNSON

Group coaching program founders need to focus on customer retention. The key to growing your year over year revenue - isn't GETTING NEW CLIENTS it's keeping them. Let's consider this, if you have 80 coaching clients at $1,000 per month for the year- and at 6 months you lose 25 of those students? That's $25k in monthly revenue lost.

Now, if you only kept 5% of those students and kept that pace throughout the year - that would be over $75k in recovered revenue (without hustling harder to find new clients). Curriculum design isn't just for starting a new program - but it's how students see success, get support, and become your biggest fan and refer you more business!

Melody Johnson is the founder of The Course Consultant. She helps visionary leaders grow their monthly and annual recurring revenue with repeat business through powerful learning experiences.

She's the podcast host of The Course Consultant Show and Certified Customer Success Manager.

8. Michael Kinney

Live-based production is a great content creation tool, but creating VODs (video on demand) should be part of every content creator's skill set. There still isn't an effective mechanism to promote or discover quality livestreams on any of the video-sharing platforms. VODs are a great way to bridge that gap.

Creating VODs that are optimized for search and suggestion on platforms like YouTube is a powerful way to introduce you and your content to new viewers. You can then push that audience to your livestreams through calls-to-action in your VODs, posts on your channel, and on social media. And VODs can do all of this relationship building, literally, while you sleep.

Game streamers are using this powerful synergy between VODs and livestreams to build large, and lucrative audiences across different platforms. Creating VODs doesn't have to be a chore for livestreamers. You can record them in the same setup as your livestream, before or after you go live. Popular livestreaming software packages, like OBS (Open Broadcaster Software) and Ecamm LIVE, offer local recording capabilities — perfect for quick, on-the-spot, "live-to-tape" VOD creation.

Michael Kinney is a YouTube creator, livestreamer, podcaster, freelance video producer, and former award-winning broadcaster.

9. Dr. Liz Isenring

I believe content and programs should be based on your passion. This is something that you are interested in or good at. It's the thing that keeps you up at night, gives you the buzz when you think about it or you find you've lost track of time when working on it.

Don't wait until the ideal time or you know everything there is about the topic. Start documenting it now. People love the journey and appreciate your thoughts. They're sick of the super slick spin that's too manufactured. I believe it's important to be real and put the content out there even if you think it might not quite be ready. Remember done is better than perfect and it's about consistent daily progress.

You attract others who are interested in the same things. Food and nutrition is my passion so I share insights about how the research is relevant to people's everyday lives, how to simplify healthy eating and of course include beautiful, colorful graphics to attract interaction and engagement.

Build up a library of relevant photos and video content and remember that repurposing is fine, as long as you take up a different angle or focus on a different point the second time around.

Most of all have fun with it. People engage with positivity, fun and inspirational content.

Dr Liz is an internationally recognized expert in nutrition and wellness and professor of nutrition and dietetics.

10. Melanie Falvey

Thanks, Ross for inviting me to be part of your book and for being so supportive towards the livestreaming and digital media community. My advice for content creators wanting to cut through the noise in 2022 would be to produce experiential content. By using all layers of communication and matching consumer behaviour trends and needs today, we can not only stand out in a saturated feed but also create more memorable experiences for our audiences.

It is no longer enough to create value-centered content, in my opinion, content marketing needs to turn into experiential marketing and livestreaming, where viewers are able to "feel" as well as consume content. Connection, entertainment, high-quality and shoppable content is where it is at. Creating a fully engaging, customer/viewer-centered experience, where they are able to feel part of something meaningful and where they can engage and shop immediately, on the spot. This is what we have been doing on Expert Channel TV for our members, we can create a cutting-edge digital brand by producing shows around their products or services as well as helping them expand into e-commerce by building a merchandise/services portfolio associated with their shows or podcasts.

Melanie Falvey is the founder of Expert Channel TV, Visibility and Authority Strategist, Video Confidence Coach, Online Communications Specialist and TV Host. She helps people become confident communicators online and host their own shows so they can show up consistently and build their authority, impact and income.

11. DANIEL J. LEWIS

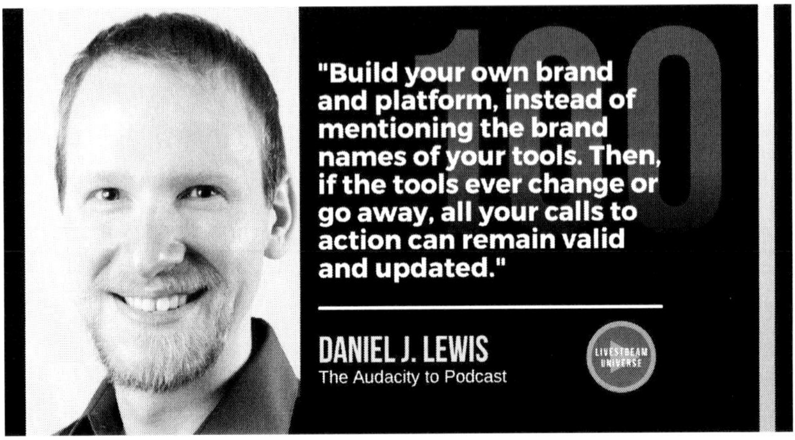

With all the new tools coming and going, I think it's vital for you to build your own brand and your own platform, instead of mentioning the brand names of your tools. Then, if the tools ever change or go away, all your calls to action can remain valid and updated.

Daniel J. Lewis helps make podcasts, podcasting, and podcasters better! He hosts the The Audacity to Podcast, cofounded International Podcast Day, create the My Podcast Reviews service, and curates data for Podcast Industry Insights. He's been podcasting since 2007.

12. Samantha Riley

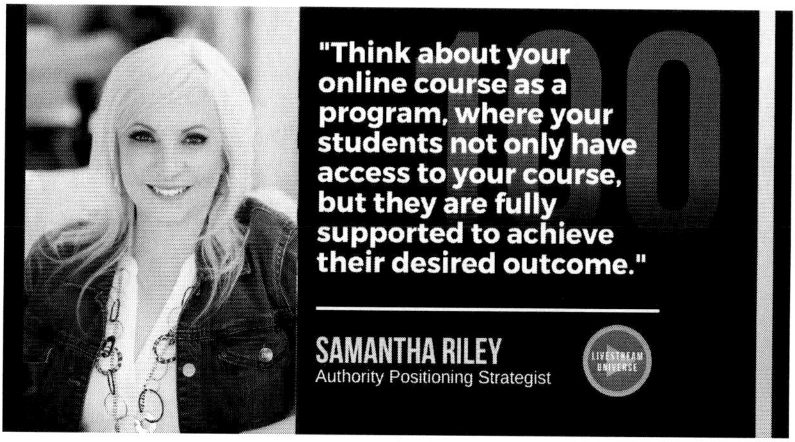

Course creation (old way) vs hybrid programs (new way): The current completion rate for online courses is only 3%. With 97% of students not completing courses, this means that course creators are not getting the success rates and subsequent case studies and referrals that they could be getting.

With the e-learning industry currently projected to hit USD $1trillion by 2027 there are many opportunities, but only if you think about course creation differently. Think about your online course as a program, where your students not only have access to your course, but they are fully supported to achieve their desired outcome.

There are 3 components to include in your program for the best results:

1. CONTENT - this is the online course or recorded modules of your course.

2. COACHING - by coaching your students along the way, you are helping them to overcome the challenges that prevent them from getting to the end of your course, and keeping momentum.

3. COMMUNITY - a group of peers to connect with for support, encouragement and connection. Your content is why they buy from you, the coaching is how they get a transformation, and the community is why they stay. Implement this hybrid model, and see your enrollments and success rates increase.

Samantha Riley is an authority positioning strategist, best selling author, speaker, host of the Influence By Design podcast and has been on the judging panel for the Stevie Awards (Women In Business) for the past two years. She has built multiple businesses over the past 28 years, and grew her first 7-figure business from the ground up before she was 30. Samantha now works with coaches and practitioners to sell and deliver their expertise online so they can live their life by design.

13. TERRY BROCK

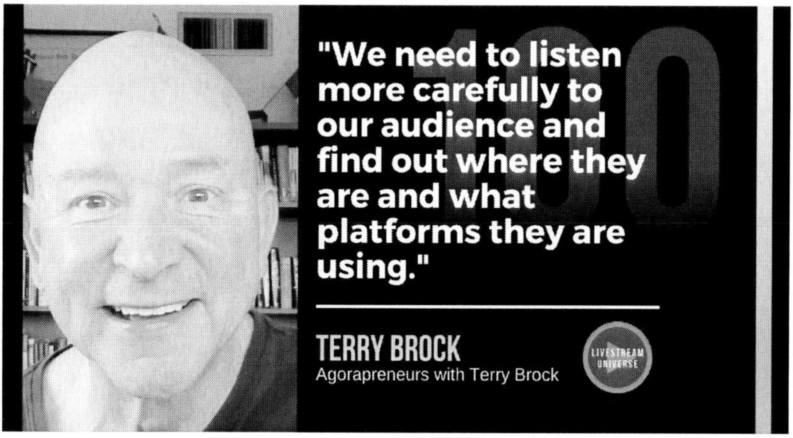

It is easy for content creators to feel overwhelmed with so many choices to use today. So what do you use? YouTube? Podcast? Livestreaming? Any of the other 500 Bazilian (actual number 🤪) choices? The answer, as always, is "The magic is in the mix." Yeah, that's good, Sparky, but what is the best mix for you?

I think we need to do what Chris Brogan advocates and that is to "grow bigger ears." We need to listen more carefully to our audience and find out where they are and what platforms they are using. And you remember all that stuff we've heard about being consistent? Yeah, it matters now more than ever so get your butt back to work and create more content you wonderful content creator! Bless you for making the world (and the Internet) a better place!

Want to understand what in blazes is going on with Web 3.0, Social Media, and more?

Terry Brock, is a Hall of Fame Professional Speaker and Marketing Advisor who shows how you can succeed in this crazy world.

14. ANNIE GIBBONS

1. **High-Quality Streams:** When you stream with a free platform or your own servers, it's difficult to achieve high-quality streaming. You need to have a livestreaming service with a robust infrastructure and a good content delivery network (CDN) to achieve high-quality video. A CDN works as a global delivery system that distributes your content using the CDN's own server. If you stream on your own, there is a high possibility that you will clog your servers. When you broadcast live to other viewers, you want to ensure that your stream works perfectly and functions consistently without any technical glitches. This is why it's wise to select a service with a reliable video streaming CDN.

2. **Greater Audience:** Potential Physical events are usually limited to the space available at a given venue. With livestreaming, however, you can invite as many people as you like to "attend" your event. Sometimes people are interested in attending a particular event, but

they can't attend in person due to work commitments or increasing expenses. Livestreaming your event can make your content accessible to these people whom you wouldn't reach otherwise. You can reach anyone in the world remotely through livestreaming, as you are no longer limited by geographical or size constraints. Your only limitation with livestreaming is linked to the server capacity of the streaming service you choose.

3. **Wide Variety of Content Use:** Live broadcasting isn't solely restricted to live video and audio streaming services. You have the flexibility to use a variety of forms of video content and multimedia, including pictures, text, and live chat. Many platforms provide a lot of flexibility to access different presentation methodologies. Furthermore, you can repurpose your live streams into on-demand content. This allows you to maximize viewership.

4. **Ease and Convenience:** A common myth about livestreaming is that it's too difficult and technical for the average person to pull off. On the contrary, livestreaming can be very simple. All you need are relevant video and audio equipment, an internet connection, an encoder, and a trusty streaming platform. Many professional streaming services provide in-depth documentation and tutorials to help broadcasters use their platforms.

5. **Analytics Tracking:** The best livestreaming services offer 24/7 customer support when you need it most. It's important to be able to track the success of your live-streamed event in terms of viewership and viewers' behavior. Most professional streaming services are equipped with tracking tools and analytics dashboards to help you evaluate the outcome of your live event. With many video

livestreaming services, you can see relevant metrics like viewer numbers, engagement, and behaviors. This data will help you to identify more clearly who your audience really is. At that point, you can assess which aspects of your broadcast you may need to change for future events. This, in turn, will help you refine your overall content and strategy.

6. **Customer Support:** It can be tricky to troubleshoot technical problems, especially if you have minimal livestreaming experience. Luckily, using a livestreaming service typically means you have access to a knowledgeable 24/7 customer support team when troubles arise. Alternatively, if you stream on your own, your only support will be Google or the information you already know about livestreaming. A reliable livestreaming service will provide you with ongoing customer support and will guide you through any difficulties you encounter.

7. **Mobile Streaming:** Most of your potential viewers likely use smartphones and other smart devices. Since consumers today view almost half of all video content online through a mobile device, the odds are that the majority of your viewers will tune in via mobile streaming. It's important to keep up with these livestreaming statistics and trends and to ensure that consumers can easily access your live stream via smartphone. Most platforms will allow you to stream your content to mobile devices and tablets through the dynamic HTML5 player, as opposed to the older Flash technology. The HTML5 video player is universal in the sense that it allows viewers to access your live stream anytime, anywhere. Using a professional streaming service gives you easy access to this type of video player.

8. **Distraction-Free Streaming:** One of the most prominent downfalls of free streaming services like YouTube is that the video player is loaded with distractions that can take away from the viewers' experience. Unrelated advertisements and third-party logos tend to clutter the screen and take the focus away from your live event. Most professional services offer ad-free streaming so you never have to burden your viewers with ads that simply aren't related to your content. Some platforms, are white-label services, which means that your live stream player comes equipped with control buttons that allow you to customize your content to your liking.

9. **Video Monetization:** At this point, you may be wondering: how can I make money from live events? Luckily, many professional streaming services are equipped with a variety of tools for video monetization. One method is to charge viewers to watch your live stream just like they'd pay for a movie or concert ticket. Viewers can pay via a pay-per-view model or a monthly subscription. A video paywall is necessary for SVOD and TVOD monetization. It restricts free access to digital content by requiring a viewer to purchase the video or pay for a subscription to gain access to the content. It's up to you to choose the payment plan that works for you and your video livestreaming goals. Many livestreaming platforms also give you the option to monetize with sponsored ads. The benefit of free platforms here is that you're in control of which ads are displayed.

10. **Reliable Global Delivery:** Most professional streaming solutions partner with powerful content delivery networks (CDNs). A CDN is a collection of servers placed strategically across different geographic regions. Partnering with powerful CDNs does more than avoid lagging and quality issues. It helps you to ensure reliable content

delivery to viewers both near and far. A CDN partnership is the best way to secure global content delivery. Some streaming services also have partnerships with the Chinese government that make it possible to stream across the Great Firewall. This clearance is difficult to get since it often requires signing papers and filing documents in China. That's why it is advantageous to use a video hosting platform that has already put in that work.

11. **Customizable Video Player:** Many professional streaming platforms support distraction-free video streaming. They allow you to stream without third-party ads or logos. However, using a paid streaming solution takes it a step further by providing a customizable HTML5 video player. Not only can you customize the branding, but you can select functional elements of the video player. It is up to you to decide what buttons and controls your player has, in addition to whether or not the player is responsive. You can set the size to fit wherever it is embedded and more. The ability to customize your video player allows you to integrate it seamlessly into the app or web page where it will live. These small things add a very professional touch.

12. **Cost-Effectiveness:** Another advantage of livestreaming with a professional service is that it is generally more cost-effective than self-hosting and investing in all of the related technology. This is especially applicable when it comes to content delivery and bandwidth. Access to a powerful CDN is expensive when you purchase it outside of a professional streaming service. CDN prices are often determined by how much bandwidth you use, so the cost can creep up on you. Since streaming services for business are typically equipped with easy-to-use features, you don't need to hire a

developer to configure things for you. Some professional streaming services are more expensive than others, but it is almost always cheaper to go with one of these pre-developed software options.

13. **Integrations with External Tools:** Although many professional streaming solutions have a wide range of features, there is a common recognition that there can always be more useful tools. The best streaming services are equipped with video API access, which allows you to customize your video hosting experience by integrating external apps and programs. This could include encoders, mixers, CRMs, and more. For example, broadcasters can integrate with Zoom livestreaming to use the web conferencing platform's peer-to-peer functionality while still taking advantage of the livestreaming service's professional hosting features.

14. **Privacy and Security:** Privacy and security are now more important than ever as piracy is at an all-time high. More than 80% of global online piracy can be attributed to illegal streaming services, with pirated video material totaling over 230 billion views a year. Free streaming platforms, like DailyMotion and YouTube, have no real privacy or security tools, so it is almost impossible to limit access to your content. Paid tools, however, are generally equipped with both privacy and security features. This keeps your content and video CMS safe from hackers and it allows you to control who has access to your video players. Some features for privacy and security include: • Password protection • Tokenized security • IP/Geographic restrictions • Domain/Referrer restrictions These tools make it possible to protect your video content from people with poor intentions.

15. **Streamlined Broadcasting Experience:** With all of your streaming tools on one, easy-to-use platform, it is quite simple to get started and streamline the broadcasting experience. Most platforms include all of the tools you need to host, manage, monetize, and deliver your content, so you don't have to jump from program to program to bring it all together.

In Summary: Livestreaming services are designed to help you broadcast like a professional and create videos that stand out to your viewers. These platforms are built for creating content that shows your audience that you are a forward-thinking and technologically savvy company skilled at implementing innovative and up-to-date solutions. Overall, livestreaming services allow you to access a broader viewer base and customize the viewing experience to meet the needs of diverse consumers. Take advantage of free trials to see what works for you.

Annie Gibbins is a passionate and purpose driven 'Fempreneur' – a CEO, Global Women's Empowerment Coach, Podcast Host, Speaker and #1 Best Selling Author. As Founder of The Women's Business Incubator, Life by Design and Women Collaborating Globally, Annie is positioned as one of Australia's leading voices for women in business. She's the CEO of Glaucoma Australia, an organization dedicated to providing sight saving education, support, and advocacy to people with glaucoma. With three university degrees under her belt, Annie is a go-to inspirational speaker globally, for women leaders in business. Her website is anniegibbons.com.

15. Mario Fachini

If you're not leveraging the power of livestreaming video, podcasting, your own YouTube Channel to sell more of your products and services whether they are online courses, virtual events, physical products or coaching...I would honestly ask yourself: "Why not?" Is there a fear of the unknown component you're battling with, or are you "gung ho" ready to dive in, and just not sure where to start? Don't wait another year to make the impact you want.

Mario Fachini is one of the most in-demand business book marketing-centric publishers in the country, having author clients that now APPLY for his training and share in the joy of creating the transformation in their businesses. He's helped clients in total generate over $1 million in new sales.

16. RJ Redden

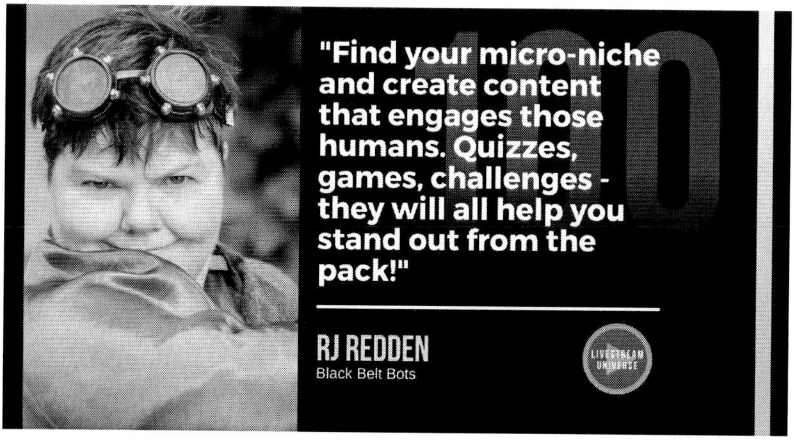

Laser target your audience. Find your micro-niche and fill it as only you can. Know their desires, fears, and what would make them ecstatically happy. This is the key. You need this key to open the door of engagement first marketing. Find your micro-niche and create content that engages those humans. Engagement: an invitation to a two way interaction. Quizzes, games, challenges - they will all help you stand out from the pack!

Coaches hire RJ to skyrocket their engagement, because most feel like they're shouting into a black hole, or they're a carbon copy of everyone else, and they can't get traction online to save their lives. RJ creates epic engagement experiences that motivate people to click that button, connect with you, and enroll like crazy.

17. Meg Glesener

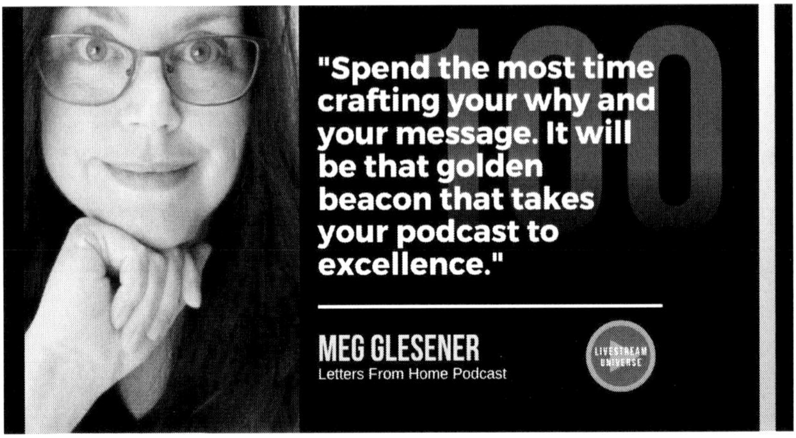

The details of podcasting can be learned. Heart, passion and drive can't. Spend the most time crafting your why and your message. It will be that golden beacon that takes your podcast to excellence. Bonus tip: add your show to directories all throughout the world. Start with these two platforms in India: Gaana and JioSaavn. Many podcasters find their audience increase by 20%. There is a world waiting to hear your message.

Meg Glesener was named to the Top 50 Moms in Podcasting in 2020 & 2021, by Podcast Magazine.

18. MIKE MURPHY

2022 Podcaster Tip: The 301 Redirect Cheat Sheet

What is a 301 Redirect?

- When moving a show from one podcast hosting company to another, you will want to set a 301 Redirect at your original hosting company to permanently forward your old RSS Feed URL to your new RSS Feed URL so you do not lose any subscribers and the podcast directories and apps get automatically updated with your new RSS Feed URL.

- The 301 Redirect is one of the last steps on your to-do list when moving a show and should only be set when you are 100% ready to stop publishing episodes at your old podcast host and start publishing at your new podcast host.

- You can think of a 301 Redirect like a change of address form for your podcast RSS Feed URL. After you set a 301 Redirect, any device, directory, app, or listener/subscriber looking for your old podcast RSS Feed URL will get automatically forwarded (or redirected) to your new RSS Feed URL.

Does a 301 Redirect move content from your old hosting company if you publish episodes after importing the show to the new podcast host?

- No. You will either want to re-import the show or manually add the episode(s) to your new podcast hosting platform.

Where do you set the 301 Redirect?

- You will enter your new RSS Feed URL in the 301 Redirect field at the podcast hosting platform you are moving away from.

How do you test a 301 Redirect to see if it is active?

- Open a web browser and paste in your old RSS Feed URL and if the 301 Redirect is working properly, then your new RSS Feed URL will open in the web browser window.

- When you publish your first episode at your new host, check all of the directories and if they update then the 301 Redirect is working and if any do not, you can manually update any directory still using your old RSS Feed with your new RSS Feed URL.

How long does a 301 Redirect last?

- Check with your old podcast host, but in most cases, the 301 Redirect does not expire and will continue forwarding your old RSS Feed to your new RSS Feed even after you delete your old podcast hosting account.

- It is best practice to keep your old podcast hosting account active for 2-4 weeks to make sure everything is working properly at your new podcast host.

Mike Murphy lives in Old Naples, Florida and is a podcaster, tutorial maker, and tech handyman who helps people figure things out.

19. Toya Glenn

The GoGiga team is prepared and ready for the future. That future is now, which is Web 3.0. A new way of transacting value has emerged with the advent of blockchain networks. Turn your content into NFT's. NFT's are digital assets for your company. It is the way you will make money from your content in Web 3.

An NFT is a non-fungible token that certifies it as unique and authentic, in combination with a buyer's virtual signature, which is backed by cryptography. It also can be used to create digital art that is collectible and creates scarcity. Whether you are an artist, musician, or business owner, digital media is the fastest way to reach your audience large scale. As a business owner you should be preparing to do something amazing in this metaverse/Web 3 space.

Toya Glenn is the CEO of GoGiga Creations, one the fastest growing black female owned digital and media distribution companies.

20. Chad Illa-Petersen

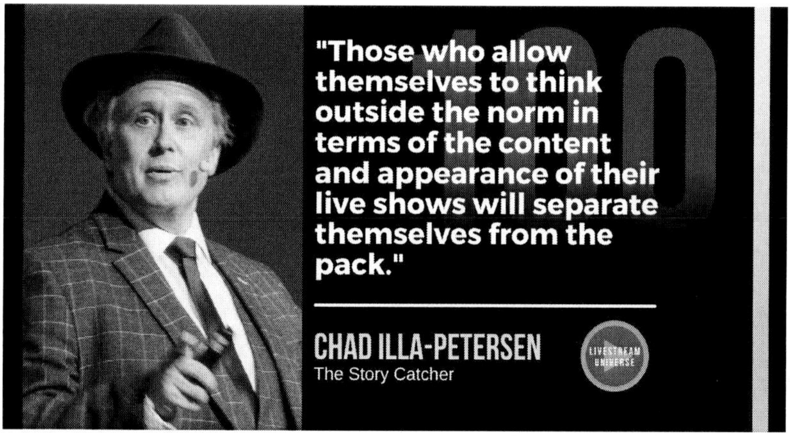

The awareness of a friend who cared changed the course of my life and placed it into a head-on collision with the world of livestreaming in the middle of the pandemic in 2020. Noticing a consistent pattern of social media posts containing hints of depression, this friend reached out and asked if I would like to start hosting a live show together hoping the new project would reenergize me. This kind act led to the creation of a show that stood out because it was different from the norm. It may not have been the best, but it was memorable.

The outside-the-box thinking of it led to opportunities to produce shows for others and my currently hosting a show for the team at wave.video. This journey and constant interaction with others in the livestreaming space opened my eyes to what I believe the industry is trending towards and craving.

Of the many ideas, feature requests, and suggestions I receive from others as well as my own beliefs around what we desire both as consumers and creators, these four stand out to me as trends, innovations, and changes heading our way.

First, I believe those who allow themselves to think outside the norm in terms of the content and appearance of their live shows will separate themselves from the pack. As we take a look at what we choose to consume and analyze, it becomes apparent that we have an innate desire to be entertained by stories, and stimulated visually. Tools that allow creators to express themselves artistically and to create a uniquely branded and recognizable show will reign. The talking head will die if it does not innovate.

Next, as the social media space becomes more and more crowded and less and less shiny, people will begin to burn out. The creator exodus from platforms due to a lack of loyalty by the social media sites that host their content will see more and more sites struggle to stay relevant. The fear of losing valuable real estate in those digital neighborhoods will see creators more frequently directing viewers to their own sites where they are more in control and can reduce the risk of being shut down by those with the "power."

However, on the reverse side of this, content platforms and social media sites will also begin to increase incentives to keep their moneymakers home. Stockholders need to be satisfied and revenues increased. In order to continue to do so, the platforms will require a constant influx of original and entertaining live content from its army of streamers and content creators. The battle to keep the best live shows on their platforms will see live streamer incentives and compensation increase.

Lastly, this desire to create live content that stands out will require the ability of creators to stream from anywhere at any time and to do so with a higher standard of quality than is currently easy to achieve at the mobile level. Streaming tools will race to be not only the first to create a livestreaming app, but also to be the best. The app that delivers the ability to have a studio on the go without sacrificing quality and at the same time allowing for visually creative components in the livestream will win.

Following a hardcore snipe hunt, botched pizzeria robbery, two years in a bear suit, and several moments atop a 6-foot unicycle, Chad Illa-Petersen (aka The Story Catcher) discovered the compelling power of stories. Today, Chad helps you find and craft the stories you didn't even know you had to create deeper connections and open a portal of belonging.

21. John Largent

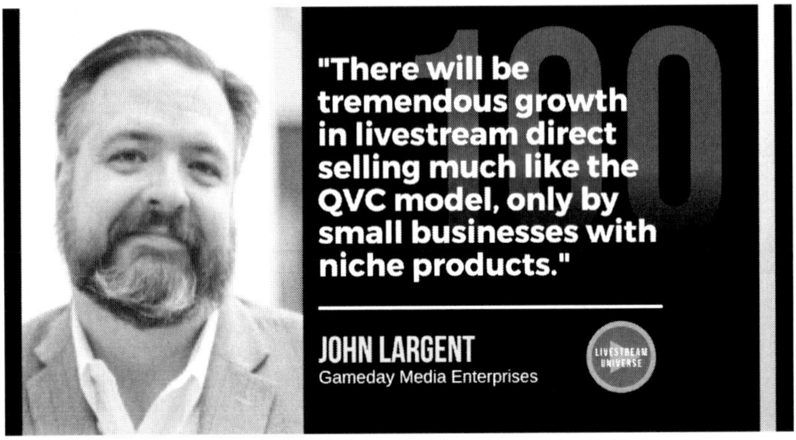

There will be tremendous growth in livestream direct selling much like the QVC model, only by small businesses with niche products. Inventors and creator will serve as their own pitchmen and will be able to answer consumer questions directly while livestreaming. All the tools exist and services like LaunchCart will make it so easy to have your own shopping network. It will be a game changer.

John Largent is the founder/CEO of Gameday Media Enterprises, an award-winning podcast production company and leading livestreaming production studio. He's been a speaker at Podfest Multimedia Expo, Podcast Movement, Outlier Festival, Texas Podcast Festival and upcoming TEDx Speaker.

22. Judi Fox

When content creators get a chance to be "early" to a new feature, it's great to take fast action. The best advice for 2022 is to watch for the launches of new features, including... LinkedIn Audio Events, Short Form on LinkedIn, Profile Video Features, and more analytics rolling out to serve you better.

LinkedIn is expected to launch a short video feature as part of Creator Mode, similar to Instagram Reels and TikTok. This short-form video feature was announced in 2021 when LinkedIn discontinued the Stories feature and acquired a tutorial video app called Jumprope. If you have been hesitating seeing LinkedIn as a place for content creators, the 2022 version of LinkedIn is powerful and according to the WSJ article "LinkedIn Might Be the Best Social Network Right Now."

Judi Fox, Founder of LinkedIn Business Accelerator, is listed as a Top 10 LinkedIn Coach for 2021 in Yahoo Finance.

Judi is featured in Inc Magazine, and speaker at VidSummit, People of Video, and Social Media Marketing World.

23. ROCKY NASH

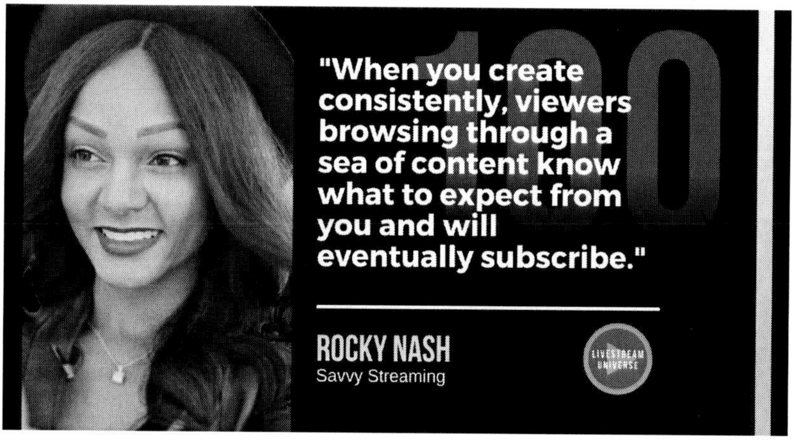

To succeed as a creator in livestream media production, I always say to start with what you have and "JUST GO LIVE!" Keep it simple, stay on topic, engage with your viewers and show up consistently. You can absolutely build a loyal online community organically. I started streaming on my mobile phone in 2015 and created new content each week until I figured it out and the technology caught up with my creative vision.

When you create consistently, viewers browsing through a sea of content know what to expect from you and will eventually subscribe. Brands started contacting me for partnerships, I participated in record-breaking marketing activations, spoke at a tech summit, attracted paid beta-testing opportunities, and even guest lectured at my local university to graduate journalism students - all before I had 1,000 subscribers on YouTube. You can make an impact as a small content creator. Years later, I was recruited to build a digital studio and produce news at a local news station. If I can do it, so can you.

1. Tell your story. You are enough and your video is exactly what someone needs to watch to be entertained, educated, or inspired. Don't compare yourself to others - focus on who will benefit from what you are sharing. That audience will show up and keep coming back because you built a safe place for them to engage.

2. Use descriptive titles because they live on when your stream ends. Someone out there will benefit from the life you've lived, the steps you've taken, the things you are proud of, and the mistakes you've made and overcome so be intentional and help them discover you.

3. Don't get caught up on the tech. We all want the latest gadget, but the best stream is one that happened. Mobile phone cameras are better than digital cameras 10 years ago, window light is great, and simple ear buds cancel out noice and amplify your voice. Upgrade when you can afford to do so - not before.

4. People will show up for mobile phone footage, but aren't as forgiving of bad audio so check for background noise and preview your stream's internet signal. Trust me on this. I've ruined great content with awful audio, but had 50k views on one of my early 360 livestreams with "acceptable" video quality.

5. Include your viewer in the conversation and ask what they want to see more of. The whole point of livestream video is to facilitate real-time engagement. Pay attention to comments and recognize those who show up every steam but don't comment. Study your audience because they are your future clients. Start today!

6. Document your experience in a way that will encourage a viewer to stop scrolling and tune in. Reassure them that your website, channel or podcast is where they belong. I am all over social media at Rocky Nash Live, but mastered one platform before branching out. Do what works for you though. You may create a new trend in remote livestream production. Yes, you! Why not? If I can make it in the industry, so can you.

7. Lastly, when you feel stuck, focus on taking the next small step, then just GO LIVE! I believe in you.

Rocky Nash is a Remote Livestream Producer, Podcast Host and VR Content Creator. As a livestream production coach at Savvy Streaming, she helps clients tell their story using immersive media platforms that facilitate building an active online community.

24. Dr. Stuart Buchan

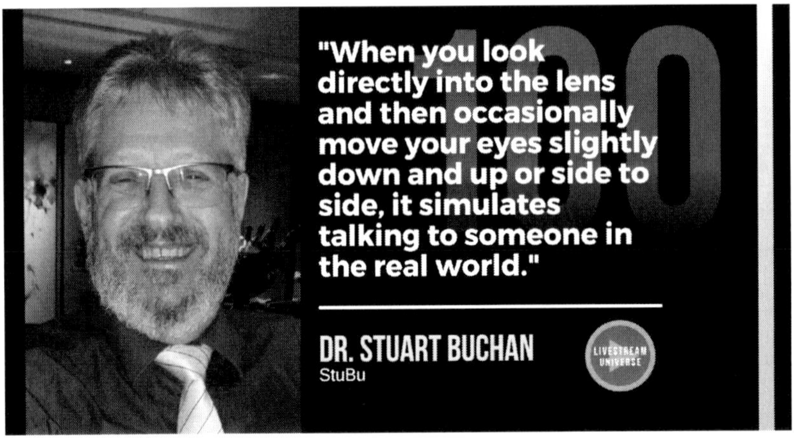

One thing that immediately hits me is: EYE CONTACT with the audience as a livestreamer, as we have a habit of looking at the screen rather than the camera lens. It's different to having a secondary camera angle in an 1-2-1 interview.

When you look directly into the lens and then occasionally move your eyes slightly down and up or side to side, it simulates talking to someone in the real world; examining their face, mouth, eyebrows, expressions, etc. Maintaining eye (lens) contact makes everything personal and intimate.

Back in 2007, Dr. Stuart Buchan began livestreaming with FirstStream as a qualified Virtual Media Consultant. It was with a Network Marketing company (VMdirect/HelloWorld). In 2017, he retired and began teaching/training/mentoring individuals, NFP organizations and companies on livestreaming on Social Media. His main focus now is promoting StreamYard.

25. Kimberly Flowers

When it comes to creating meaningful and valuable content for your audience, I think it's important to remember that your message can be made more impactful when in collaboration. This year, be on the lookout for other like-minded content creators and brands in your industry who have fundamentally similar objectives for why they create and consider doing a show or podcast together. If you are not techy but want your show to have a professional custom brand look, consider working with a remote producer. Working together with a few other influencers and tech experts will definitely help lighten the creation workload, and with all of your promoting one platform it will be easy get more eyes on your broadcast and ears on podcast!

Kimberly Flowers is the founder and CEO of Remote Producer Live!, a remote production company specializing in the production of online TV Shows & Virtual Events.

26. Paul Brodie

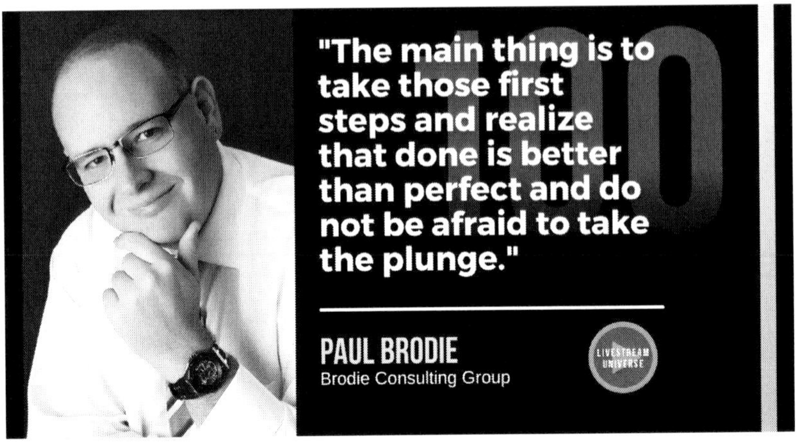

The best advice I can give is to just do it. Whether that is writing a book, hosting a virtual summit, or giving a live webinar, the main thing to do is to just get started. Lao Tzu once said that the journey of a thousand miles begins with the first steps. The same applies to any of these ventures. The main thing is to take those first steps and realize that done is better than perfect and do not be afraid to take the plunge. You will be amazed what happens to your life both business-wise and personally when you do take those first steps.

Paul Brodie helps people share their story and position them as an expert in their field. At Brodie Consulting Group, we accomplish this by launching our clients books to a guaranteed best seller (we have done 68 consecutive best-selling launches in all genres), turning our clients manuscripts into a great looking book, or by positioning our clients as the Oprah in their industry by hosting and launching a virtual summit.

27. ANTHONY "LAS CURRY" SANTANA

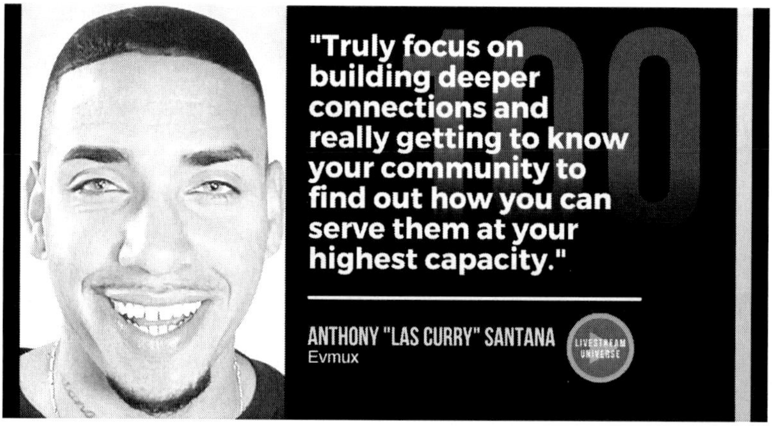

The advice that I have for content creators in 2022 is to really lean into building a deeper and more meaningful connection with their community. The best way to be able to achieve that is by not only utilizing livestreams and short form content but to focus on storytelling! I truly believe that the year of 2022 in content creation is really going to dive deep into building more connections and telling stories. Whether it be stories to be able to entertain, to be able to inspire, or to be able to educate.

It's going to be important that we as creators start to be more transparent, more vulnerable, and really showcase the good and the bad of content creation. I think gone are the days where we create this fantasy world on social media. Viewers, audiences, and consumers want to feel relatable to creators and have more meaningful connections with them. I truly believe that the creators who lean into livestreams that provide a more realistic and interactive setting to be able to connect with their viewers but also lean into storytelling will win big this year!

Final thoughts for 2022 are to go ahead and start livestreaming if you haven't already and figure out ways you can incorporate your community into your content and into your story. Truly focus on building deeper connections and really getting to know your community to find out how you can serve them at your highest capacity.

Anthony Santana is the head of content at Evmux and a livestreaming expert who helps creators and entrepreneurs grow their brand and influence online using live video.

28. NICK MATTINGLY

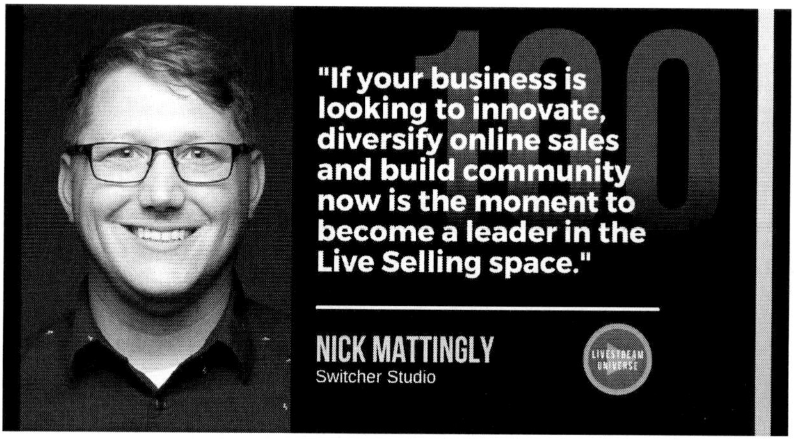

Video Commerce and Live Selling are big business in Asia. These trends are just now starting to take a foothold in other markets. If your business is looking to innovate, diversify online sales and build community now is the moment to become a leader in the Live Selling space.

Nick Mattingly is the CEO & co-founder of Switcher Studio. He's an industry thought leader, speaker and social video expert building the storytelling platform of choice for creative businesses and teams.

29. Doc Rock

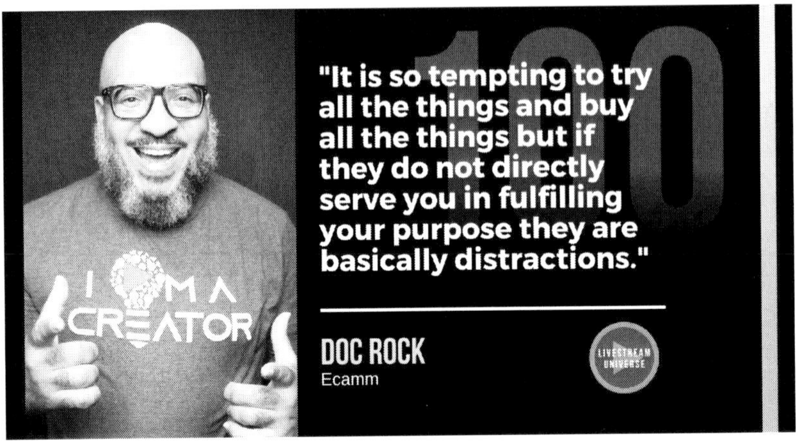

Find your purpose as soon as possible and do the things that move you in your purpose. It is so tempting to try all the things and buy all the things but if they do not directly serve you in fulfilling your purpose they are basically distractions. Intent and purpose are the keys. What is your intention and are you purpose driven?

Bonus tip: Yes, YouTube will be doing podcasts soon so be 100% ready when that time comes.

Doc Roc is the community manager for Ecamm Network. He believes your community is most important, subscribers and followers are vanity metrics without community, and Ecamm's amazing community is hands down its best feature.

30. Beth Granger

My advice for reluctant content creators, or those that think they have nothing of value to share, is to start by answering the top frequently asked questions you receive.

Your content can start in the format that is easiest for you: written, image, or video, but you will want to experiment with different formats to see what your audience or network likes.

Don't be afraid to "get real." I once shared my blooper reel of all the out-takes I didn't use when making my LinkedIn Cover Story video.

Observe the content you consume that makes you stop and think, or inspires you. What about it attracted you? Was it a good story? Beautiful image? Was it inspirational or educational?

That will guide you on the type of content to create.

Beth Granger is the CEO of Beth Granger Consulting: Intrepid Social. She works with organizations, individuals, and leaders who want to grow their business or professional brand by unleashing the power of LinkedIn.

PART IV
RESOURCES

NEXT STEPS

Thank you for choosing this book. Don't forget to get your free book bonuses at:

livestreamuniverse.com/readerbonuses2.

These include special offers and discounts on great products for livestreaming and online business. If you'd like more help in creating content that serves your audience and builds your business, we have you covered:

1. **Subscribe to the #StreamLeader Report**: Our free monthly report delivers livestreaming and digital media tips, tools and trends to keep you ahead of the competition.

   livestreamuniverse.com/streamleader

2. **Participate in the Monetize Livestreaming Now™ Facebook Group:** Share your expertise and get answers to your questions about livestreaming and business in our free Facebook group.

   facebook.com/groups/monetizelive

3. **Monetization Masterclasses:** Accelerate toward your content and business goals with our training videos covering all aspects of monetization from email marketing to brand deals. Includes access to 20+ masterclasses.

   monetizelive.vip

LIVESTREAMING & VIDEO CREATION SOFTWARE

Live Video Production & Streaming

StreamYard: Popular livestreaming and video production app for beginners and a strong choice for live video hosts and producers at all levels of experience. **livestreamuniverse.com/streamyard**

Ecamm Live: All-in-one, easy-to-use, high-quality video production and streaming tool for Mac. **livestreamuniverse.com/ecamm**

Melon: Brought to you by the team behind Streamlabs, Melon empowers creators to livestream with ease. Pro Plan includes high-quality local recordings with separate video and audio tracks and a teleprompter feature. **livestreamuniverse.com/melon**

Switcher Studio: Leading choice for mobile live video production using iOS devices. Sync up iPhones and iPads for multi-cam video, insert titles and graphics, edit live, and stream anywhere.

livestreamuniverse.com/switcherstudio

Wave.video: This video marketing platform has added its own livestreaming studio with everything you need to host, produce and multistream your own live shows. **livestreamuniverse.com/wave**

Evmux: Game-changing features including a fully customizable pro-scene builder, iso recordings, multiple local cameras, talkback and concurrent broadcasts. **livestreamuniverse.com/evmux**

Wirecast: Stream like a pro with complete control over the look of your broadcast.

livestreamuniverse.com/wirecast

Video Editing & Screencasting

ScreenFlow: My go-to video editor has a completely new UI — refreshed for macOS Big Sur with a new customizable toolbar, reworked preferences windows, improved timeline track functionality and main menu organization.

livestreamuniverse.com/screenflow

YouTube Optimization

TubeBuddy: The best tool for growing your YouTube channel by helping you identify growth opportunities while optimizing your videos for success. Free Chrome browser extension.

livestreamuniverse.com/tubebuddy

Video Sales

Uscreen: Sell videos online with the world's leading video monetization platform. Own your audience, customize beautiful themes, sell courses and much more.

livestreamuniverse.com/uscreen

Video Overlays & Backgrounds

Streamer Templates: Stand out on live video with customizable templates designed specifically to work with StreamYard's layouts.

livestreamuniverse.com/templates

Transcripts

Otter.ai: AI transcripts of audio and video Content.
livestreamuniverse.com/otter

VIDEO GEAR

Links to video gear below at

kit.co/rossbrand/video-gear-recommendations.

Webcams

Logitech C922x: If you are using your computer's built-in webcam, upgrading to these external webcams from Logitech will greatly improve the quality of video.

Logitech C920: A top webcam choice of live streamers for years thanks to its reliable video quality, the Logitech C920 typically costs less than the C922x while delivering similar results.

Mirrorless Cameras

Sony a6400: When it's time to upgrade from a webcam, the Sony a6400 is my choice thanks to its superfast autofocus, clean HDMI output and unlimited recording time. Amazing low light performance.

Green Screen

Elgato Green Screen: Transport yourself anywhere in a moment! A rocksteady solution optimized for camera chroma keying, Green Screen sets the stage for truly immersive broadcasting in a matter of seconds. Ideal for even the tightest workspaces.

Lighting

Viltrox LED Light Panels: Lighting is critical for good-quality video. These small, light-weight and portable LED light panels have adjustable intensity and temperature. Get the AC adapter with it so you don't have to worry about charging when livestreaming.

Capture Card

Elgato Cam Link 4K: Connect your DSLR or mirrorless camera, camcorder or action cam to your computer so that it appears as a webcam. Plugs directly into USB slot so an additional USB cable is not needed. Great value.

Multi-Camera Switchers

ATEM Mini Pro: Connect up to 4 HDMI video cameras, switch shots and output as a single USB webcam feed. Blackmagic includes multiview and streaming directly from device to social media in the Pro version.

ATEM Mini: Offers the same 4 HDMI camera inputs and high-quality video output as the Blackmagic Pro version at half the price, but without the multiview and direct-to-social streaming.

Remote Livestreaming Hardware

LiveU Solo: This portable video encoder creates consistent bandwidth and a reliable connection for livestreaming from even the world's most bandwidth challenged environments. Create high-quality, remote broadcasts with one-touch, directly from your camera source.

AUDIO GEAR

Links to audio gear below at

kit.co/rossbrand/audio-gear-recommendations.

Studio Microphones:

Shure SM7B: The mic I use in my untreated home studio and one of the elite dynamic mics for radio, podcasting and livestreaming. Versatile, warm and sounds good on many voices. Looks nice on video, too.

Electro-voice RE20: My favorite microphone when I worked in radio. I still revere the clean, classic broadcast sound of the RE20.

Heil PR40: Another high-quality microphone option for broadcast, podcast and streaming.

Electro-voice RE320: More affordable than the RE20 and has enough output to work with consumer interfaces.

Shure MV7: It's the best sounding USB dynamic microphone I've ever heard and it's great with the XLR cable too.

Elgato Wave:3: If you don't want your mic on camera, this USB condenser mic picks up quality sound without much extra noise.

Samson Q2U: This is the USB mic I recommend for people starting out.

Remote Handheld Interview Microphone

Electro-voice RE50: Industry standard for ENG (electronic news gathering). Ultimate remote interview microphone with low handling noise. Unsurpassed ruggedness and reliability in every environment.

All-Purpose Microphones

Sennheiser e835: This dynamic XLR mic can serve a lot of use cases without hurting your budget. It is a capable studio host or guest mic, an excellent option for handheld interviews and on-stage use and a light-weight travel companion.

Shure SM58: The classic on-stage mic, it shines in a multitude of environments and use-cases including home recording and streaming and handheld interviews.

Audio Interfaces, Mixers & Recorders

Sound Devices MixPre-6: A spectacular audio interface, mixer and recorder for studio and remote work. Outstanding preamps and analog limiters. Legitimate pro gear. Expect a learning curve.

Rodecaster Pro: One of the best options for podcasters and livestreamers with excellent audio quality. Cool features include 4 headphone amps, pads for playing sounders and built-in processing options.

Zoom PodTrak P4: Compact, affordable, and loaded with features, the PodTrak P4 makes it easy to capture professional audio wherever you are.

Microphone Boom Arms

Rode PSA-1 Boom Arm: This is the sturdy boom arm I use to hold up the heavy Shure SM7B microphone. Great for home studios with large broadcast-style microphones.

Neewer Mic Boom Arm: An inexpensive tool to keep your handheld style mic off your desk, at a comfortable height and out of the way when the broadcast is over.

Headphones

Sony MDR-7506: These professional studio headphones are popular with podcasters and livestreamers. Used for editing and not as bulky-looking as other options when seen on video.

Sennheiser HD 280 Pro: Bulkier than the Sony MDR-7506, some people find the 280 Pro set to be a comfortable choice for longer studio production sessions.

GRAPHICS & SHORT VIDEOS

Streamer Templates: Stand out on live video with customizable templates designed specifically to work with StreamYard's layouts.
livestreamuniverse.com/templates

PlaceIt: Create mockups, logos, social posts and videos in seconds. Great for intro videos for livestreams.
livestreamuniverse.com/placeit-2

Wave.video: Create thumbnails, backgrounds, overlays, intros, outros and other image and video assets to use in your content.
livestreamuniverse.com/wave

Depositphotos: High-quality stock photos and video b-roll.
livestreamuniverse.com/depositphotos

Creative Fabrica: Fonts and design elements for your online graphics and physical products.
livestreamuniverse.com/creative-fabrica

Canva: Popular DIY graphic design platform.
livestreamuniverse.com/canva

VistaCreate: A strong alternative to Canva, VistaCreate offers high-quality templates and even a photo background remover tool in the free plan.
livestreamuniverse.com/vistacreate

WEBSITE, EMAIL & MARKETING

WordPress

Elementor Builder: Build and customize every part of your website intuitively with Elementor's visual builder. Zero coding required.

livestreamuniverse.com/elementor

Elegant Themes: Divi is the most popular premium WordPress theme in the world and comes with Divi Builder.

livestreamuniverse.com/divi

searchditto: WordPress plugin that helps you get your audio and video content found and consumed by more people. Give a new life to older content.

livestreamuniverse.com/searchditto

Podcast Website

Podpage: Build a beautiful podcast website in five minutes from your RSS feed.

livestreamuniverse.com/podpage

Domains

NameCheap: Tends to have lower prices than its competitors along with a beautiful website and easy-to-use interface.

livestreamuniverse.com/namecheap

Email Marketing

ActiveCampaign: Email list building on the world's leading email automation platform.

livestreamuniverse.com/active

AI Copywriting

Jasper: Quickly create online content with AI copywriting optimized to convert.

livestreamuniverse.com/jasper

Media Kit

OneSheet: Easy media kit for creators.
livestreamuniverse.com/onesheet

Course Delivery & Sales

Thinkific: Popular choice for building online courses and membership communities.

livestreamuniverse.com/thinkific

EPILOGUE

I had no idea what to expect when I published the first book of predictions in 2021.

One thing I certainly didn't predict is that there would be a second volume within a year featuring 100 more predictions.

While I was confident in the value of the predictions, insights and advice submitted annually by our esteemed panel of creators and entrepreneurs for the Livestream Universe blog, I wondered… would they work in a new format for a wider audience? And, if it could possibly work, how would a self-publishing rookie make it happen?

It's common knowledge that publishing a book is challenging. Even knowing that, many new authors will tell you it's much harder than they expected.

Once I was done gathering 100 contributors, transcribing hours of audio, cleaning up nearly 50,000 words of transcribed text, creating hundreds of graphics, spending many sleepless nights trying to design two different options for book covers, running through multiple attempts to format the text I had so far while continuing to add more content, learning about Amazon KDP, rebuilding my email list from scratch and coming up with the marketing content, it was almost time to launch.

Not so fast. I wasn't sure that my best efforts – weeks of all-nighters to design the cover and format the text – met the professional standards I wanted for my first book. Fortunately, I have a good friend in Dale L. Roberts who is an expert in self-publishing. So I started to do a deep dive into his books, YouTube videos and blog posts. Thanks to Dale's experience with a wide range of designers and formatters, I ended up with excellent recommendations to outsource the two tasks that were holding up progress. The superstar responsible for both book covers is Danielle Camorlinga.

After gaining a fundamental understanding of KDP through Dale's content. I benefitted greatly from working with him directly to tailor his publishing strategies to my book.

Meanwhile, Jennifer Quinn aka JennyQ dropped a beautifully-written foreword that left me speechless.

I was excited that publication was finally close at hand.

Once again, not so fast. The formatting of the book had major issues. The free tools I had used while attempting to format it myself, when exported as a Word document, didn't maintain the paragraph breaks or image placement.

Once the formatting was done, the amount of content in the book made it necessary to publish in a larger size paperback than expected. That meant the cover – which I now know you should never do before the formatting – needed to be revised for the new dimensions.

Fortunately, those problems were solved and I still had a couple days left until launch. Phew.

The next day when I went to upload the ebook to KDP and set the pricing, I was in for a shock. I had publicly promised to set the price of the ebook for 99 cents for launch day. Emails were sent and graphics posted on social. But the file size of 89 MB was too big to sell for 99 cents according to Amazon rules. The lowest price allowed was $2.99.

Attempts to decrease file size got us as low as 20MB, but no lower. Either I had to raise the price or miss the launch. Unless... I took out some of the images.

The night before launch I didn't sleep at all. First I dropped the pull-quote graphics that were in most chapters. Still too big. Then out went the screenshots of the people who delivered their predictions on video – the overwhelming majority of the entries. I got it down to 1MB and the price dropped from $2.99 to $1.99.

If I was going to make good on my promise to sell for 99 cents, the only option left was to publish the ebook without images. I removed all 100 graphic quotes at the top of each chapter with the contributor's photo. Finally, I could set the price to 99 cents. Amazon approved the ebook by late morning of launch day and before the clock hit Noon ET, the paperback and ebook went on sale.

My greatest hope for launch day was that a few people would buy the book so that it might show up on the Amazon charts, at least long enough to snap a screen shot that would begin to slightly validate, in my own mind, the time and money invested in this project.

Before long, Dale messaged me a screen shot of the book at #1. And then it went to the top of another category. Minutes later, I saw it ranked first in another category.

By the end of the first 48 hours, the book hit #1 on the Amazon Best Seller rankings in 17 categories. Both the ebook and paperback versions reached #1 in multiple categories. It even entered the top 5,000 in all Kindle ebooks sold on Amazon.

The reception blew me away. There were five-star reviews on the Amazon sales pages. #100Predictions would go on to receive six book awards.

Another aspect of the launch that helped was adding email outreach, thanks to everything I was learning from #FtheHustle newsletter publisher Kim Doyal's success with her list.

While the first book's content came primarily from a five-hour livestream that included back and forth conversations with the contributors, this time there were no audio files to transcribe. All the predictions in this second book were delivered in writing and the chapters belong entirely to the contributors.

The 100 all-stars who contributed to this book and the 7th Annual Livestream Universe Predictions.

However, this volume goes beyond the first one in other ways. In addition to the 100 predictions by 100 top creators, 30 additional influencers add their expert advice and tips for digital media creation in 2022.

I've also expanded the resources section at the back of the book to include my recommendations for livestreaming hardware and software, audio and video gear and tools to help with marketing, graphics and more.

Our second round of entries features 30 additional creators and entrepreneurs sharing strategies and advice exclusively for inclusion in this book.

Thank you for reading. I'd love to hear your thoughts on the book as a whole or any of the topics we covered. You are welcome to chat with me directly on Volley at **talk.volley.app/ross** and join our Livestream Universe space on the app.

You are also invited to continue the conversation with many of our contributors in the free Monetize Livestreaming Now™ Facebook Group at **facebook.com/groups/monetizelive.**

Ross Brand
Livestreaming Video Host & Strategist
livestreamuniverse.com
talk.volley.app/ross
facebook.com/groups/monetizelive

ACKNOWLEDGEMENT

First and foremost, a huge thank you to good friend and self-publishing expert Dale L. Roberts for going above and beyond to help make the first #100Predictions book a #1 Amazon Best Seller and six-time book award winner. Your videos, books, resources and advice – as well as your vast knowledge of the self-publishing industry – helped deliver results well beyond my wildest imagination. I'm honored that you took time to contribute the foreword to this book.

Thanks to Vincent Suppa of HR Avant-Garde. You are a loyal friend, a trusted colleague and one of the most brilliant business minds to ever work in the HR profession.

Thanks to author and fellow introvert Nancy Ancowitz for your friendship and advice. It's always a joy to share ideas with you and to benefit from your knowledge of the publishing and media industries.

Thanks to author and livestream pioneer Jennifer Quinn aka JennyQ, who wrote the previous volume's foreword. We've shared this livestreaming and digital media journey since you were a guest on my very first show. You are one of the best hosts to ever work in the medium and I love how you've been embracing podcasting. Your friendship and continued support mean the world to me.

Thanks to the multitalented Rachael Anne Clifton aka @BeautyBubble for generously sharing your input and wisdom whenever asked. You have a genius for helping to shape promising ideas into concrete concepts. I can't even begin to count the number of times I've seen you support others to elevate a project with your strategic insights and keen attention to detail.

A special thanks to five amazing people who contributed to this book and were part of the first Predictions blog post. In addition to the aforementioned JennyQ, Jennie Mustafa-Julock aka Coach Jennie, Mitch Jackson aka The Metaverse Lawyer, Tim McDonald and Mark S. Babbitt all provided predictions in late 2015, only a few months after Livestream Universe had launched and little more than a month after my first show. Thank you for the leadership you bring to our community and for your friendship over many years.

Thanks to author, email marketing superstar and #FtheHustle newsletter publisher Kim Doyal for pushing me to use email to promote the first book. Your advice on putting together a sequence for the first book launch was invaluable to its success.

Thanks to Winnie Sun for insisting I co-host your Monetize Livestreaming Now session, turning it into a fireside chat that received many positive reviews from attendees. Thanks as well for having me on your terrific Nasdaq TV show, Level Up with Winnie Sun.

Thanks to author, livestreamer and Hollywood insider Joie Gharrity. You've been such an enthusiastic supporter of the predictions since we connected on a virtual Social Media Day event in 2018. It's been a joy to collaborate with you and I can't wait for our next project to shine the spotlight on talented creators.

Thanks to Jon Burk of Al Roker Entertainment for touting the predictions across the industry and inviting some great contributors to participate without me even asking. From the Never Settle Show to Web Summit and the first book launch, your kindness never waivers and your sense of humor makes it all a lot more fun.

Thanks to podcasting royalty Dave Jackson and Jim Collison for being the same down-to-earth, friendly and helpful people offline that you are on your podcasts and livestreams. Thanks to audio legend Chris Curran for being as funny and genuine off-mic as you are in the recording studio.

Thanks to talented creator and friend Michael Kinney for embodying the best of what it means to be a professional broadcaster.

Thanks to Online World Summit for Livestreamers founder Anita Sonya for always promoting my shows and content.

Thanks to Dealcasters' hosts Jim Fuhs and Chris Stone for arranging a surprise book launch show for the first volume featuring many of the book's contributors.

Thanks to some of the leading livestreaming brands for choosing to work with me. I have enjoyed hosting shows for StreamYard, BeLive and LiveU and serving as a brand ambassador for Telestream Wirecast.

Thanks to the industry brands who have sponsored shows and events, including, but not limited to, generous support from Uscreen and StreamYard for the first Monetize Livestreaming Now™ Virtual Summit in 2021.

Thanks to Hannah Jacobson and the team at Book Award Pro for all you do to support authors.

Thanks to Danielle Camorlinga for designing the outstanding book covers in this series.

Thanks to Sue-Ann Bubacz for sharing her editing suggestions that helped make the book better.

Thanks to the Advanced Reader Copy (ARC) Team for providing pre-publication feedback and launch day outreach: Jeffrey Fitzgerald, Ileane Smith, Brad Friedman, Sue-Ann Bubacz, Stuart Buchan, Coach Jennie Mustafa-Julock, Terry Johnson, Chad Illa-Petersen, Bridgetti Lim Banda, Jim Fuhs, Gord Isman, Dr. Aikyna Finch, Jeff Sieh, Jim Mullen, RJ Redden, Alec Dorling, Rocky Nash, John R. DiStefano, Jr. and David Simon.

Thanks to all the contributors to this book for sharing your insights and expertise. Each of their names appears in the table of contents and at the top of their chapter.

And last but not least, thanks to my parents for always being my rock. I love you.

ABOUT THE AUTHOR

Ross Brand is an award-winning livestreaming strategist with a dedicated following among digital influencers. He's served as an on-air personality for industry brands such as Streamyard, BeLive and LiveU and a brand ambassador for Telestream's Wirecast.

Ross was selected one of "5 Live Video Experts to Follow" by Switcher Studio, the "Number One Twitter Account for Learning Live Stream Marketing" by Amp Live, and a Top 25 Video Marketing Influencer by Onalytica. He's been featured by Psychology Today, Nasdaq TV and Forbes. Klout ranked him the world's #1 livestreaming expert on social media.

Relevant Links:

Website – livestreamuniverse.com

Twitter – twitter.com/irossbrand

Instagram – instagram.com/rossbrand1

LinkedIn – linkedin.com/in/rossbrand

YouTube – youtube.com/livestreamuniverse

Facebook Page – facebook.com/livestreamuniverse

Facebook Group – facebook.com/groups/monetizelive

Send Ross a message:

talk.volley.app/ross

DOWNLOAD FULL COLOR EDITION FOR FREE

As an additional thank you for getting the book, I'd like to give you the full color digital version 100% FREE!

DOWNLOAD at **livestreamuniverse.com/fullcolor2**.

Made in United States
North Haven, CT
10 November 2026

22106136R00146